# Becoming the Church

# Becoming the Church:
## Lessons for Today's Disciples

Dalton Troy Rushing

Copyright © 2012 Dalton Troy Rushing

All rights reserved. No part of this publication may be reproduced or transmitted in any form or by any means, electronic or mechanical, including photocopy, recording, or any information storage and retrieval system, without permission in writing from the copyright owner/author.

Speaking requests and requests for duplication or distribution may be addressed to Dalton Rushing at dalton.rushing@gmail.com or 678-404-0378.

All scripture quotations from the New Revised Standard Version Bible, copyright 1989, Division of Christian Education of the National Council of the Churches of Christ in the United States of America. Used by permission. All rights reserved

ISBN: 1481257137
ISBN-13: 978-1481257138

*For Stacey, my partner in life and ministry*

# CONTENTS

|    | Introduction             | ix  |
|----|--------------------------|-----|
|    | How to Read this Book    | xi  |
| 1  | And What Now?            | 13  |
| 2  | Peculiar People          | 19  |
| 3  | Stand Up and Walk        | 25  |
| 4  | The Limits of the Church | 33  |
| 5  | You Must Choose          | 39  |
| 6  | Change                   | 45  |
| 7  | Peace                    | 51  |
| 8  | Not Magical. Powerful    | 55  |
| 9  | The Courage of Ananias   | 61  |
| 10 | When the Spirit Moves    | 67  |
| 11 | In the Face of Tragedy   | 71  |
| 12 | Worms                    | 79  |
| 13 | The "E" Word             | 85  |

| 14 | On Seeing God | 91 |
| 15 | Church Business | 97 |
| 16 | God's Justice | 103 |
| 17 | The Importance of the Mind | 109 |
| 18 | You Don't Graduate from Church | 115 |
| 19 | Planting Seeds | 121 |
| 20 | The Long Story of God | 127 |
| 21 | Radical | 133 |
| 22 | You | 139 |
| 23 | Resistance is Real | 145 |
| 24 | The Consequences of Integrity | 151 |
| 25 | Going It Alone? | 157 |
| 26 | Truth to Power | 163 |
| 27 | Shackled Leadership | 167 |
| 28 | The end? | 171 |

# Introduction

The Christian Bible is a holy, difficult, confusing, enlightening book. In fact, the Bible is not just one book. It is a series of books, all ultimately written about God, but with different authors, themes, styles, and aims.

With such a diversity of books in the Bible, it can be difficult to just pick up the Bible and figure out what God is calling us to do today. Even the most recently written books of the Bible were written nearly two thousand years ago, and while some books of the Bible are clear about how we should live, other books do not appear to be about us at all.

Because the Bible is so complex (more complex than we sometimes give it credit for), it is no surprise that churches and Christians all over the world have very different understandings of what it means to follow God, even though we are essentially all reading the same Bible. Figuring out how to be a disciple today, two thousand years after Jesus walked the earth, is difficult business. The world is so different than it was in Jesus's day. I have no idea, for instance, what Jesus would think of the Internet. Following a savior who lived long ago is not easy.

As we look the Bible to teach us how to live, let me share two pieces of good news. The first piece of good news is that we do not have to figure out how to be Christian by ourselves. In fact, one of the core messages of the Bible is that you cannot just pick up a Bible and go live as a Christian by yourself. The founder of my religious tribe, John Wesley, is quoted as saying that "'Holy solitaries' is a phrase no more consistent with the Gospel than holy adulterers." We are made for one another, and when we ignore the fact that we must do this work together, we are ignoring much of the Bible. If the Bible belongs to anybody, it belongs to the whole church, and we are called to figure this all out together.

The second piece of good news is that we are not the first ones to try and figure out how to live as Christians without Jesus available for questions and answers. The Book of Acts tells the story of the first disciples, as they struggled to figure out how to use the broken shards of their community after the Resurrection of Christ in order to fashion a new way of living. They had to become the church.

You and I continue this work of becoming the church today. In many ways, we are like the first disciples, stepping out into a strange land with a strange message about a strange savior. The Book of Acts is an excellent guide as we step out in the same faith as did the early disciples.

# How to Read This Book

*Becoming the Church* is a book to be read alongside the Bible. Each chapter of this book corresponds with a chapter in the Book of Acts. You are encouraged to begin by reading the corresponding chapter in Acts, meditating upon its meaning, and then following up your scripture reading by spending time in this book.

At the end of each chapter, you will find reflection questions relating to the message presented in that chapter. While this book can certainly be read alone or in one sitting, I would encourage you to try reading one chapter a day. Then, find a conversation partner to discuss the reading and your own reflections. In the tradition of the early church, reading the Bible should be done in community. God's truth is most often revealed in conversation with others.

BECOMING THE CHURCH

# And What Now?
Acts 1

*As they were watching, he was lifted up, and a cloud took him out of their sight.*

And what now? Perhaps there is no such small question with such large implications. Something ***huge*** has happened, and naturally, there must be a response. But what now, when you must continue living after an event so important that time is bursting with preparations, filled with getting ready and making arrangements, and then, all of a sudden, the thing is over, and what now?

    New parents stare at their infant daughter in the delivery room. Her nursery in their home is painted a fresh pink, and new linens line her crib. Doctors are dithering about, and the child's family is waiting in the lobby for news, but what are the new parents to say? "It's a girl," of course. Yes, it's a girl, but yet, she is so much more. She is so much more than her gendered self, so much more than her tiny body. She is the sum total of her parents' hopes for themselves and for the world. She is ready to be filled by what her parents have to teach her, and yet she is somehow already full. She is so much more than just a girl, but her parents have not prepared for the enormity of what has just happened. They have spent so much time preparing for her arrival, so much time with the paint brush and the credit card, that they have no idea what to do now.

The baby's father walks into the waiting room and says, "It's a girl." This is what you say, after all, when the child is a female. You accept the cigars and smile, because there is nothing in language to express the size of this moment, no words to express such hope. You fall back on convention, as it is all you have.

And so it is for the apostles, the early disciples of Jesus. In the Resurrection, they have seen the bounds of space and time ripped to shreds in front of their eyes, such that nothing will ever, ever be the same.

"Nothing is impossible with God" goes both ways, of course. You can't implode the laws of nature—as in, he was dead but now he is alive—without some ill effects. Nothing is sure. There is no stable ground. And if Jesus had been the one thing on which they had been relying, well, now that was gone, too, and there was thus no longer a human yardstick by which to measure experience. There was only a hole, a vacuum, a lack-of-Jesus.

They gathered. This is what you do when something momentous has happened: you gather. And so they did, "Peter, and John, and James, and Andrew, Philip and Thomas, Bartholomew and Matthew, James son of Alphaeus, and Simon the Zealot, and Judas son of James . . . constantly devoting themselves to prayer, together with certain women, including Mary the mother of Jesus, as well as his brothers." One hundred and twenty people were there in total, milling about and wondering what to do next. There had been so much time spent with Jesus, so much time following him, and preparing for the cross. But he was gone now.

It seemed to Peter that what they needed was a meeting, an election, to fill the spot Judas left behind after dying on the land he bought with the reward money for Jesus's capture. There had been twelve, now there were eleven, so they cast lots to fill the spot.

But why worry with something as simple as an election, when the earth had shaken and Jesus had died and risen again? There were eleven apostles left, after all. Why replace the one? Surely, eleven were enough.

## Lessons for Today's Disciples

The election of Matthias was *wholly* unnecessary. There were plenty of apostles left, and when *those* apostles were killed, one by one, nobody thought to cast lots to replace them. But after Jesus's death, casting lots gave the apostles something to do. After the preparations, once the event has happened, all there is to do is keep going, to take the next step and then the next, until you are walking again. You go back to what you know. So they had an election, because it was all they knew to do, and once it was over, they went on from there.

If this is something with which the apostles struggled after Jesus's death, then the struggle is only more difficult today. With uncertainty becoming more and more a fact of life, we look for something—anything—against which to measure our lives. When war threatens our way of life, we cling to nationalism as a way of making sense of events. When social norms change, we talk about the way things used to be better. When the church declines, we talk about metrics. And when we are presented with religious questions which shake the core of our faith, we ignore them, for they are simply too difficult for us to bear. Instead, we become increasingly rigid in our faith, unwilling to challenge ourselves.

We refuse to ask the important questions. Did God cause this to happen to me? How can a loving God allow something like this? I have tried to be faithful; what more does God want from me? How might God be calling me to change? How can I be expected to be in communion with all these people from around the world, when I cannot even get along with my neighbor next door?

The questions are altogether too difficult, and we are already in full mourning over life's uncertainty. There is neither time nor energy for questions, and so our wounds are left to fester. This festering, we seem to believe, is preferable to engaging questions which challenge our faith, which challenge our Church and the structures of our lives, and so we continue to ignore the questions. They are simply too difficult.

It is much easier to talk about God's "plan" than to ask serious questions about God's role in our lives, God's role in the world and in the Church. So we simply do not ask. Ignorance, after all, is bliss.

But this response is not good enough, for it is fear-driven rather than faith-driven. God is bigger than this ignoring of difficult questions. God is much bigger than our questions—we acknowledge this—but yet we do not allow God to be the subject of our questions, as if questioning God would somehow bring down the whole framework of heaven and earth, as if our blind, unthinking loyalty to God were what God most desires, as if the fact that we have brains were an accident.

In the final analysis, I have to believe that it is not the questions we fear, as much as it is the answers. Ignoring the questions is easier than bearing jagged answers, so we do that.

In times when nothing seems sure—when the Messiah has risen, when the child has been born, when the church has been floundering—we need a roadmap more than ever, because we are not even sure of which questions to ask, not that we had the intestinal fortitude to ask in the first place. We need a guide, something to call to us from the liminal space between the wilderness and the promised land.

Thankfully, the church has been given the gift of scripture so that we do not have to wander alone. Scripture tells the story of God's people; Jesus's life, death, and resurrection; and some of what happened after Jesus. It can be the last part that is the most helpful in unsure times, as scripture tells the story of a people scared and confused and hurting and lost and frustrated . . . and doing their best to be faithful.

Acts is the story of what happened to the church *after* Jesus. The apostles—and the rest of Jesus's followers—had to continue on, somehow, and make sense of what Jesus had taught them. The Book of Acts is a gift to us, as it shows us that though the apostles did not have all the answers, they did the best they could with the hands they were dealt. The apostles, having finally prepared for Jesus's death, were left with the empty tomb, forced to figure out how to continue to be God's people in the world. Acts is their story.

The church does well to reread Acts every now and again, and as the religious and cultural landscape changes more and more quickly these days, we need Acts now more than ever. We need not reenact what happens in this book. Simple reenactment is no more faithful a witness than ignoring the difficult question of faith. Nor should we get bogged down in the cultural differences between the time of Acts and today's society; Acts is the story of the apostles, not the story of today's church. And yet there are important lessons to be learned, because the struggles of two thousand years ago appear in today's church in only slightly varied forms.

Who belongs here? How can we hold this together? Where do we go from here? What now? These questions, asked by the apostles after Jesus's death, continue to be important for the church.

This is the story of Acts: that the apostles, faced with a world in which Jesus was no longer physically present with them, had to figure out what to do next. The Book of Acts is the story of a group of people, dedicated to God and fumbling towards becoming the church. The apostles have experienced something which will not allow them to live as they always had. Their experience demands a response. And just as they have experienced God, so have we. Perhaps we have not experienced God in such vivid terms. But the Christian life is, at its core, about experiencing God and figuring out what to do next. This is the work of becoming the church. Though the apostles began this work, it is yet unfinished.

We live at a time in which the future of the church is unsure. We are sure of God's power and grace, but we do not know what God's church is going to look like in the years ahead. We are at a crucible moment, and we have work to do, so let us fumble along with the apostles. Let us be their partners in this important work.

## Questions for reflection:

1. The times we live in are difficult. They are much different from the times of Jesus. If Jesus walked into your home or church today, what do you think he would say?

2. Think about a time in which you were unsure about what to do next. How might faith in Jesus help you move forward?

# Peculiar People
Acts 2

*But others sneered and said, "They are filled with new wine."*

Church people are strange folks. We believe—most of us anyway—that two thousand years ago, a man-God died and arose from the dead. From the inside, belief in the resurrection makes sense, as we live in a church culture that largely accepts this premise. But think about the implications of this event, from a modern, scientific perspective. There is simply no proper explanation. On its face, this peculiar belief is enough to render most of us certifiable, but the eccentricities, of course, continue beyond the issue of the resurrection.

Consider the Lord's Supper. We have differences on how we understand the Lord's Supper, but the sentiment is more or less the same. And even if we do not consider the ritual of taking Communion as literally eating the body and blood of Christ (as some branches of the church do), we believe that the bread and wine represent the body and the blood. Consider this for a moment. In quite a literal sense, we celebrate cannibalism each time we take Communion. Charles Wesley's hymn, "Come, Sinners, to the Gospel Feast" goes like this:

# Becoming the Church

*Come and partake the gospel feast,*
*be saved from sin, in Jesus rest;*
*O taste the goodness of our God,*
*and eat his flesh and drink his blood.*

Truly, we are strange folk.

Yet we accept these strange customs as normal. "Of course," we say, "this is just what Christians do." And when someone dares to challenge the custom, we cling to these customs as if they were Jesus himself, and we dare not let go. Thinking of Communion as cannibalism is offensive, of course, as partaking of the Body and Blood of Christ involves so much more than it may appear; the Lord's Supper is a gift from God, of course. My denomination, the United Methodist Church, talks about Communion as a "means of grace," which means that God works through Communion to build our faith, to strengthen us and commune with us. I do not mean to suggest that Communion is merely a custom, but the fact of the peculiarity of the sacrament remains.

So we do well to remember that we are a peculiar people, each community, each individual, each in our own way. The church, having become culturally dominant (particularly in the southern United States), glosses over this peculiarity, such that there is a "new normal" within the church. We have our own ways of speaking, of dressing, and of being the church. Even our experiments in broadening the definition of church are becoming stereotyped. We have biker churches, praise music, and tattooed youth ministers, and we accept these changes as a "new" way of doing church, when often, our new methods are recycled: worn and threadbare and an excuse to argue that the church really is relevant, when all we are doing is looking like has-been fools.

No, we are a peculiar people, but we have trouble seeing that we are peculiar, because we have created our own new way of understanding normal. And as peculiar as we are, if someone is not peculiar in the narrow way we allow, we ignore that witness completely, because *this is The Church, after all, and there is a certain way we do things around here.* All too often, the church expresses willingness for peculiar people, only to limit the kinds of peculiarity allowed inside its doors.

I remember hearing once about a booming church, full of young people: people who didn't really fit anywhere else, but not fitting in was ok, because it was *the church*, after all, and the church was where people who didn't fit could go and feel like it was ok not to fit.

Those are the kind of people who went to that church: young women with short hair and young men on motorcycles, and it was great, great for everybody, until one Sunday, when it came to the pastor's attention that one of the young women with short hair had returned after several months, and she had brought her newborn child with her. If she had been married, of course, the whole church would have cooed at the child, would've told mom just how much the baby looked like her, but since she wasn't married, there was none of that.

They marched her right up the center aisle during worship that Sunday, they stood her in the front of the church, and they had a vote right then and there as to whether someone who gave such a bad name to the church belonged there.

And who cares whether they voted to keep her or to reject her, because no matter how they voted, the verdict was passed the moment they made her walk up the aisle. Of course, they were just doing their job. She had upset the holiness of God's church and something just *had* to be done about it! But they broke right in two; the congregation and the town and that poor young woman broke right in two.

That young woman brings us quite directly to the doorstep of Acts 2, because if there is one group the church need not fool with, it's the drunks. We know there is nothing worth hearing from the drunks. One wonders just who the apostles think they are, babbling on at nine in the morning as if sailors on leave. In his defense, Peter tells the crowd that it is far too early for drunkenness, as if there is a proper hour for such debauchery: as if the nine o'clock hour will prove his sobriety. I have seen enough people with paper bags in the morning to know better than to blindly accept this excuse.

Whether or not the crowd takes him seriously at first, we do not know. They probably gather to rubberneck, to watch the spectacle of twelve drunks trying to string sentences together. But before long, as Peter quite coherently quotes the prophet Joel, and as he recites a psalm, the crowd—mostly Jews who know this scripture, too—warms to him.

It takes only the recitation of scripture, and the crowd warms to him. But these days, people come, scripture in hand, with a word for us, and we dismiss them quickly without listening. The question becomes: does this person fit one of the standardized profiles of abnormality recognized in the church? If a person fits the profile, we put him up front on Sunday morning and let him tell his story. But if such a person is outside the bounds of what the church has deemed acceptable, there is no use for her. She need not waste her breath.

Over the years, the church has missed out on many truths because these truths have come from those who are poor, or homeless, or with disabilities: as if these descriptors are de-facto pejoratives, as if we automatically assume that there is something wrong with being poor. When did the standard of capitalistic success become the standard by which we judge people? When did conforming to some societal norm become the standard? We are peculiar people! We should expect peculiar people among us!

It is not such a far leap to imagine a version of Christianity which becomes little more than a tool for success, a church which exists as a vehicle for professional networking rather than the place where Christians come together to figure out what calling ourselves "Christian" really means.

But what a potential we have, if we simply listen to those peculiar voices! Because the crowds in Jerusalem were willing to listen to the twelve, the Day of Pentecost ended with three thousand people being baptized. And if baptism is not enough, those three thousand people—having listened to those they assumed to be drunk—lived from that day forward as changed people, selling everything they had, helping those in need, sharing meals, and praising God.

We focus so much on the miracle of the tongues of fire—earth-shattering, though it is—that we miss out on the other miracle of Pentecost: that though the apostles seemed to babble on drunkenly, people listened to them anyway.

These days, of course, we have it under control. We don't need to do anything so drastic. We have exactly the kind of people we want. There is no need for people who are, you know, different: those who seem full of new wine. This is the church, after all.

## Questions for reflection:

1. Many times, those of us in the church have ignored peculiar people in order that we may reach out to those with whom we feel the most comfortable. Who are some of the people who need the Gospel the most? Why has the church not reached out to them? How might the church include them in God's saving work?

2. Who are the peculiar voices in your life? What might you learn by listening to them?

BECOMING THE CHURCH

# Stand up and Walk
Acts 3

*And he fixed his attention on them, expecting to receive something from them.*

The first story of healing after Jesus's ascension is the story of the man paralyzed from birth. This story does not appear in the Revised Common Lectionary, the schedule of scripture readings used in worship by most Christian denominations. There are too many stories in scripture, of course, to include all of them in the three-year cycle of the lectionary. Some things must be left out; some books of the Bible do not appear in worship readings at all. Churches who depend upon the lectionary will never hear the Old Testament Book of Ezra read in worship, nor the New Testament's Epistle of Jude, nor several other books and stories. Three years is just not enough time to include everything, so the church necessarily leaves some things out.

Still, there is something unsettling about leaving out the story of the man lame from birth, as this is the first Biblical evidence of the apostles knowingly using the power of God. The tongues of fire just *happened* to them, of course. The drunken babbling of Acts 2 was beyond their control. But in Acts 3, Peter purposefully offers healing to the man stretched out in front of the temple. Peter has no alms, of course. The outstretched man is looking only for money, but

Peter has sold everything he has. He has no alms, nothing to give except healing, and so healing is what he offers this to the man.

While this story is not included in the lectionary, the rest of the chapter—Peter's speech in the temple—is read as part of the normal cycle, as if Peter's explanation is good enough. The church seems to be saying, "Who needs to see the healing when Peter gives a perfectly good explanation?" But one cannot get the full effect from the speech, of course. A book review is not the same thing as a book; a recipe is quite different than a meal. The church has lost the immediacy of the healing; we have taken the joyful, childish skipping of a grown man and turned it into a polemic on repentance.

It is a shame that the church does not claim the story of the man lame from birth for its worship, because there are times when it seems as if the church, knowing that there are no alms coming, does not even look up from the mat. Why waste the effort? It is a difficult world, and sometimes the burden of life seems so heavy that lifting the head is the hardest possible thing to do.

Yes, sometimes it is difficult to have faith, but in these times, we do well to read this little healing story, because as a whole, the third chapter of Acts tells us something very important about faith. Each of the two parts is important; Peter's speech is just as important as the healing. But viewed together, there is an important lesson about the nature of faith and belief that the church ought to heed. The lesson comes from Peter, who seems to say two very inconsistent things.

As Peter and John enter the temple to pray, they notice a man lying at the gate of the temple, begging for alms. They have surely seen this man before; he appears daily, as his friends lay him there to beg. This man's life is consumed by begging. He does nothing else. He can do nothing else. Surely, Peter and John have seen this man before, since they are regulars at the temple.

But this day, rather than pass this man by, something spurs them to speak to him. "Look at us," they say. As the man turns to receive a coin, Peter reaches down to take his hand. What a wasted gesture this is, taking the man's hand. He cannot walk and probably cannot feel the touch. No matter. Peter takes the man's hand anyway, and Peter says, "I have no silver or gold, but what I have I give you; in the name of Jesus Christ of Nazareth, stand up and walk."

And the man does not just walk; he jumps! This is a joyful man, and of course he can do nothing but praise God, as he is no longer relegated to lying in front of the temple, left behind by his friends like a broken down car on the side of the road, and unable to do anything but beg.

Everyone is amazed; they have seen this man day after day, begging for money and unable to do anything else. Perhaps he was faking, they must ask. But no, he has been there far too long, endured the sun for far too many days to be faking. This is real, and they are amazed.

But Peter, sensing that the crowds see him as a magician, defuses the situation. The power of healing comes not from Peter and John, but from God. "Why do you stare at us?" Peter asks, "as though by our own power or piety we had made him walk?" Peter is not powerful enough to heal—only God can do that—and there is no level of piety high enough to make him (or anybody else) capable of playing God. It is not Peter and John who have healed the man; they have offered God's healing.

This is where Peter says the inconsistent thing. Peter says, "The faith that is through Jesus has given [the man lame from birth] this perfect health in the presence of all of you." And we have heard this kind of thing before. Luke, who wrote both the gospel that bears his name and the Book of Acts, tells the story of Jesus healing the ten lepers, and suddenly, that story sounds very familiar. It is all very familiar, as Jesus heals the ten lepers, sends them to the temple, and one of them cannot help but run and jump and praise God. And Jesus tells the leper, "Your faith has made you well."

The leper that Jesus healed has the faith, of course. It is after the running and jumping and praising that Jesus says, "Your faith has made you well." And the lepers sought out healing from Jesus; they approached him and said, "Jesus, Master, have mercy on us!"

But the man lame from birth had sought out no such healing. There was no healing to seek. He had never walked, never known the feeling of wet grass on his feet. This was a man whose world was sideways and low to the ground, and his body was of no use to him. How could this man seek healing when he had no idea what it meant to be well? This man was a piece of furniture, to be set out each morning and scooped up each night, and if being immobile was not enough, he was forced to beg from the dusty ground. His faith could not make him well any more than he could get up and walk. He knew neither wellness nor faith. There was nothing to know.

Yet, Peter says, "The faith that is through Jesus has given this man this perfect health." Surely, Peter knows that the man lame from birth has no faith in anything other than his own immobility. In what would he have faith? For what is there to hope? The man wants money. That is all. He hopes for money, not for God.

The man turns his head toward Peter and John as they prepare to enter the temple, and he asks them for money. He has no idea who they are; he has no faith to speak of, and yet Peter says that the man has been healed by faith.

But perhaps it is not this man's faith that has healed him. Perhaps Peter and John, seeing a man who is unable to have faith of his own, have enough faith to go around. Perhaps these two apostles, knowing that this man has been laid on the ground so many times that he probably does not even see himself worthy of walking, have compassion on him and offer healing in the name of Jesus Christ.

Is this really such a revolutionary concept, this sharing of faith? It certainly goes against the Westernized notion that faith is an individual decision, to be placed upon the human heart and hidden with flesh and bone, never to be doubted. When I am asked "Have you accepted Jesus as your Lord and Savior?" I answer "yes," of course. But imagine asking this question to the man lame from birth! Go to the temple gates, crouch down on the dusty ground, and ask the man: Have you accepted Jesus as your Lord and Savior? Ask him, because the answer you will get will be a firm "no." When there is seemingly nothing to have faith in, and the burdens of life keep you down, how can you be expected to answer any other way?

Have I accepted Jesus as my Lord and Savior? If I am honest, there are days so filled with pain that at best, my answer is "yes, but . . ."

Faith is not something you simply have or you don't, of course. When doubts come, we feel that we are being unfaithful, as if we are cheating on God and flirting with trouble. But doubt does not discount God! The good news of Acts 3 is that even in times of doubt—even when the world seems to conspire against us and we can neither get up from the mat nor lift our heads—faith can make us whole again. The theologian Paul Tillich has written, "Doubt is not the opposite of faith; it is one element of faith."

I heard a minister tell the story of a prominent family in his church. This family was the wealthiest in town, giving extravagant amounts of money to the church and the community, participating in worship and volunteering for their Saturday morning soup kitchens. When this new minister came along, the church was resistant to him, as tends to happen with new ministers. But the family embraced him, trusting that God would use him in a way that would please God and help the church grow. These were good people, loved by everyone in the church.

And on Saturday evening, as the minister worked on the final bits of his sermon for the next morning, he received a phone call from a church member. There had been a tragedy. The family's private plane had crashed, and there were no survivors. The husband and two young children were dead.

The minister struggled with what to say about the tragedy. He stammered through his sermon the next morning, unsure about how to go on in the face of such an awful experience. And he spent hours in front of his Bible and computer as he tried to write the funeral sermon. He would speak of the man's business accomplishments, of course, and of the delightful sounds made by the children as they ran through the hallways of the church. He knew of the goodness of this family, and so he had much to say about them. What he struggled with was explaining the goodness of God in the face of this tragedy. He knew what to say, of course; he had spoken in many a funeral service. But in this service, in a tragedy that struck him in the center of his heart, he had trouble believing.

The funeral sermon came together, of course. The sermon always seems to come together. But it was not the sermon that served as the most powerful element of the funeral service. The surviving family, sitting on the front row, was as heartbroken as you might expect; I heard someone one once say that the only proper response to the death of a child is to roll over and play dead. And the sermon was nice, but it did nothing to alleviate the sorrow of this family. You cannot explain death; you can only talk about it. And with such tragedy on display that day, how could the family be expected to have faith?

As the minister counseled the family in the days after the funeral, he learned that it was the Apostle's Creed that proved most helpful to them that day as they dealt with their grief. Those gathered for the funeral filled the pews and stood in the aisles, and at the appointed time, they spoke the words of the Apostle's Creed. "We believe in God, the Father Almighty, maker of Heaven and Earth."

And though the family, in the wake of such profound grief, could not have been expected to believe in God on that day, the entire group gathered surrounded them with this historic affirmation of faith. It was, the minister said later, "as if the congregation, knowing of the doubts carried by the family on that day, believed *for* them until they could believe again."

If that is not a good model for what the church should be, I do not know what is.

## Questions for reflection:

1. Have you ever felt so low that you could barely raise your head to ask for help? When?

2. How might the church reach out to those who have barely enough faith to realize that they need other people? How might you reach out in your own life?

## Becoming the Church

# The Limits of the Church
Acts 4

*Now the whole group of those who believed were of one heart and soul.*

This passage seems outdated, past its expiration date, curdled and needing to be tossed out.

No one pools their resources any more, after all. The church is just not institutionally able to support something like that. Sure, perhaps when Peter and the apostles were around, it made sense. They did not have much to begin with, so they put everything together and did the best with what they had. But only the craziest religious sects do something like pooling resources these days. The church as we know it is just too big for something like that, and the people in it just not able to drop everything and divest. We have mortgages to pay and children to feed and, well, it is just not feasible. This is not to mention that we have seen how communism works, which is to say not at all. So we forgive Luke for his shortsightedness in describing this practice, but communal living will simply not work anymore.

Think out the implications of selling everything and living communally. First, when the housing market is down, and a Christian's home mortgage is underwater, selling everything and moving to a commune will not satisfy the bank. We have responsibilities, of course, and we need the car to get the kids to basketball practice, and we need the money to buy birthday cards, and we need to save for retirement so that we do not end up flipping burgers at the age of eighty. It is unfair to Luke to blame him for this confusion, since this chapter was written two thousand years before the invention of the Roth IRA, but it remains that we have to deal with a passage that simply does not make sense for us anymore. What are we to do? Do we simply ignore the passage? Surely, there is good news to be found within it, but Luke just asks too much of us.

One minister whose words I appreciate says of this passage that it is awfully discouraging to preach a message you know will be ignored. I think that is right. The work of a preacher is hard, and when this passage appears in the lectionary, the preacher cannot just ignore it. The preacher cannot ignore it, but everyone else is allowed to, or at least that is the implication, because the claims of the passage are just too bold. The church simply cannot so radically adapt to that which is being called for in Acts 4. It would collapse upon itself, leaving debris everywhere. This idea is just too bold.

I am not just talking about possessions. Sharing of possessions is what the end of this chapter is about, of course. But Acts 4 is no mandate for socialism. There is no directive to live just this one way in order to please God; thankfully, God seems to love us no matter the economic structure under which we live. So while Luke seems a bit naïve in his description of how the early Christians lived, he does not say that one must live likewise to be a proper Christian. That is a load off.

The problem of this text is not just about possessions. The problem is mostly about community, that sharing of ourselves (and, on occasion, our possessions) that leaves us open to one another and ultimately vulnerable: that is, vulnerable in an ultimate sense, completely exposed and forced to share this exposed-ness with those with whom we are in community. And if I am honest, I must admit that this vulnerability is *much* harder than selling all my possessions. If I sell everything I own, after all, I still have me. But if I am radically vulnerable, and if I share of my most human humanity, then parts of me are stripped away such that I do not have any idea what will be left.

Yes, selling my home and everything else is easier than that, no matter my mortgage bill. And no matter how long I sit with Acts 4—no matter how many times I read it, and in how many translations—Luke is clearly talking about something which I am simply unable to do. I would more likely sprout wings and fly.

Not that the apostles had it any easier than we do. Luke tells us about this communal living in the same chapter that he talks about Peter and John being imprisoned. This is their first imprisonment, at least as far as Luke tells us. We tend to whitewash the New Testament prison stories, as if what the apostles were really doing in jail was knitting socks. Prison is a dismal, damp, uncertain place, particularly when you are arrested for no reason whatsoever and your leader has just been killed.

These were no specially trained people, either. Peter and John had spent time with Jesus, of course, but they were essentially laughed out of court because of their lack of credentials. These were "uneducated and ordinary men," not the kind of folks on whom you would stake the future of humanity. So they let them go: told them to be quiet and let them go, because they were too uneducated and ordinary to do no harm.

What great acts came from these uneducated and ordinary people! Imagine if we expected such acts from the ordinary people who make up the church. The church is full of ordinary people, and if we expected the ordinary church do to extraordinary acts all the time, perhaps we would not be so concerned about keeping the church from falling in on itself, because we would be more concerned about the ministry being done! Perhaps we would worry less about what was impossible and worry more about seeing to it that all of God's children are being cared for.

Peter and John, who do not have the proper schooling, understand that it is not simply education that determines excellence. This is not to put down education; God works in education just like

God works elsewhere, and if there is one thing the church needs right now, it is good, educated leaders. But education is not the end-all, be-all of Christian life. Education is a means to more effective leadership: an expression of God's love through preparation. But Peter and John lack this requirement altogether, and it seems that someone forgot to tell them, because they continue on as if they had God on their side.

Somehow, the scene with the religious leaders does not exhaust the apostles; they are ready for more. And rather than retreat to lick their wounds, the apostles pray for boldness. Gluttons for punishment, the apostles know quite well that praying for boldness means. This is no naïve prayer; this is the prayer of people profoundly affected by the love of God, educated or not. Theologian Karl Barth says that the only prayer that God will always answer in the affirmative is the prayer for more faith, and for Peter and John and the rest of the bunch, this prayer for more faith means more than an extra ounce or two of devotion. This prayer for boldness is a death wish, and they know it, but there is far too much at stake to play quietly. There is far too much at stake in the world than to lick their wounds and retreat.

The question becomes, is there less at stake now? Has technology, and modern medicine, and higher education, and the electoral process, and the food pyramid—have they all rendered us able to quit depending on God? This must be the question, because to visit worship nowadays is to watch a community absolutely sure that they will be there again the next week, with no need to worry about how they will get there. Nothing is at stake any longer. We have lost the immediacy of the Gospel, and we have certainly lost the vulnerability that comes with opening ourselves to God and one another. The church does not pray for boldness, because it does not want to have to deal with the consequences of being bold.

But when boldness happens, amazing things result. A rich landowner sells everything he has and gives the money to the poor. Two former prisoners continue to preach the Gospel, knowing all the while that they will be arrested again, and again, until finally they are put to death. And a group of believers, having prayed for boldness, peels back the layers of nonsense and pretense that surrounds the core of our humanity, sharing who we are with one another.

If this means that the church falls in on itself, so be it. We will worship together on top of the rubble.

## Questions for reflection:

1. Think about your own faith. Have there been times in your life in which you have ignored difficult truths because they were inconvenient for you?

2. How might the church take more seriously God's call to boldness? What is one way in which you or your church can be bolder?

# You Must Choose
Acts 5

*He fell down and died.*

Here is a story about a man who gave nearly all of himself to God. He awoke early each morning and prayed for an hour before breakfast, he prayed for an hour before bed, but he saved a few minutes a day for himself, and he dropped dead. Some men took his body and buried him. The dead man's wife came in to see what the commotion was about, and she dropped dead, too.

This seems more like a vaudeville act than New Testament Bible story. Oh, we might expect something like this in the Old Testament, with its bear maulings and forbidden fruit and dry bones. But we are past this now, and the New Testament is no place for such foolishness.

So the first question we must answer is that of what this story is doing in Acts in the first place. The story of Ananias and Sapphira does not fit the rest of Acts. Theirs is no monumental act, and this story seems notable for nothing other than the surprising outcome. The rest of Acts details grand actions on the part of the apostles and their followers, but this story zeroes in on these two mostly-believers. In the grand scheme of Acts, the story of Ananias and Sapphira is decidedly off-off-Broadway.

This is a surprising little story, and naturally so. We do not expect such harsh punishment for something as benign as keeping a part of ourselves from God. And so this story is equally shocking, because we are forced to deal with not one, but two deaths. We must figure out how something as everyday as keeping part of the proceeds from the sale of a field makes Ananias and Sapphira deserve death. After all, have they not just done something incredible, selling their land and giving nearly all of it to God?

This is a difficult passage with which to work, because Ananias and Sapphira have given so much more than we do. This is much easier understood as a Biblical oddity—look at that funny story. Isn't it interesting?—rather than a story that has profound implications for the life of the church today. After all, I have yet to sell my land and give most of the proceeds to the church, and if death is what greets those who give nearly everything, imagine what greets those who give the minimum ten percent!

Only, we do not give ten percent. Some of us do, of course. There are those saintly folks among us who give and give and give. But we do not give ten percent. Most studies of tithing in the United States suggest that on average, we give about two and a half percent of our incomes to the church. Two and a half percent! This makes me think that pastors who prattle on about tithing should lower the bar and just ask everyone in the congregation to give three percent. Imagine what the church could do with an extra one-fifth of the church's operating budget! The ministry we could do! Only five percent of Americans tithe, anyway, and even that figure is not quite right, because that study counts charitable groups in with the churches.

Our giving is dwarfed by that of Ananias and Sapphira. Even those who boast that they give fifteen or twenty percent of their income to the church have little ground to stand on in light of this story. And for the rest of us, if we cannot manage to give three percent of ourselves to the church, how can we possibly expect to stand before the apostles, having laid our gifts at their feet, and walk away unscathed? Asked another way, when was the last time we trembled as we put a check in the offering plate?

Naturally, times are different now. There is no longer the expectation that we sell everything we own and give it to the church, and perhaps this expectation was not around in the apostles' time, either. After all, if that expectation was there, Barnabas's generosity in Acts 4 would not be such a big deal. Barnabas's act was big enough to make it into the Bible, and I would think that is a pretty good standard for judging whether something is a big deal. So Ananias and Sapphira's troubles cannot be traced to the fact that they did not give a hundred percent. There must be something else that makes Ananias and Sapphira's gift cost them their lives. There must be something else that makes the less-than-a-hundred-percent gift an unfaithful one.

The problem is less about the large gift that they did give, as it is the small part that they did not give. The problem is that in this act, Ananias and Sapphira chose to keep part of themselves from God. This is not the same as only giving *most* of the proceeds from the fields. Ananias and Sapphira went to the apostles and laid their donation at their feet, as if this extremely generous act would give them a leg up in the community. But the question remains: why keep a small part for themselves? Why not just give the entire amount of money, rather than keeping just a bit?

The money they kept served as insurance, in case this whole Jesus thing did not work out. Why else would they keep it? It was not as if they did not have enough food to eat; the field which they sold was not their only property, and there was enough money in the communal pot for food, anyway. No, this is the only explanation: that the small part they kept back was for "just in case."

The only reason for skimming some off the top of such a large gift is for insurance, in case Jesus is not who he says he was, and this all calms down in a few years. Act like you are giving it all, make people think you are committed, but stock a little away for a rainy day.

Skimming off the top is not trusting in God. This kind of religious insurance is exactly the opposite of trusting in God: making arrangements so that if God does not deliver, you are not stuck in a bind. Ananias and Sapphira may be doing the same thing as Barnabas in that they have sold a field, but they are doing the exact opposite of Barnabas in that they are putting their trust in themselves.

And this is the problem with Ananias and Sapphira's gift: it is not so much a gift as it is a public presentation with an insurance policy attached. There is nothing trusting about this gift; it is for show. In fact, this is not so much a gift at all, as it is a putting-of-eggs-in-different baskets, you know, just in case. This is not a gift at all, because God calls us to trust, completely, because there is no other way to trust. Taking some off the top, just in case, leaves God with an incomplete person with which to work, and there is too much at stake for us to be incomplete people.

There is too much work to be done. Either the church is full of incomplete people, and will fail, or the church is full of complete people and nothing—not Gamaliel, nor Caesar himself—can stop us. The choice is this simple, between completeness and incompleteness, between yes and no.

This is the message of Acts 5: if you give your entire self to God, even prison bars will be unable to keep you contained.

But give an incomplete version of yourself to God, and you might as well be dead.

If you do try to hitch your wagon to two different horses—if you do try to give God an incomplete version of yourself—do not be surprised when they pull in opposite directions and they rip you apart.

## Questions for reflection:

1. Where does your ultimate allegiance lie? How do other parts of your life get in the way of worshiping and following God?

2. So many times, the church seems to give into culture rather than living out the faith we were given in Jesus. How can we make a step towards being more authentic in our faith journeys?

# Change
Acts 6

*What they said pleased the whole community.*

In the place that I live, there have been several violent storms in recent days. We seem to be the only home in the neighborhood that has not lost a tree, and we consider ourselves lucky. It is sad really, when trees that have been around since before the area was even developed fall in a storm. Trees seem permanent. We climb their branches as children, we carve our initials in them as young lovers, and we rake their leaves year after year in a season-changing ritual. I know someone who talks about his favorite tree on the college campus on which he teaches as if the tree were an old friend, roughed by the years and the weather but sharing the experiences of his life for the last twenty-some-odd years.

With apologies to Shel Silverstein, a tree stump leaves much to be desired; I can sit on the ground, thank you very much. There is just nothing good about a fallen tree.

Fallen trees are what I have been seeing in my neighborhood for the past few weeks, and they nearly all the same. The saying is true: the bigger they are, the harder they fall. It is the largest trees that lay strewn across yards and streets, that are left propped up on roofs and power lines. It would seem that because the bigger trees have more expansive root systems, they would be the strongest in the storm, but this simply is not true. The smaller trees, with the less expansive roots, always stay standing, while the largest trees in the neighborhood—those trees which have overseen years of neighborhood life—fall and crush everything in their path. Those expansive root systems pull straight up out of the rain-sodden ground, leaving upturned dirt all around.

No, there is just nothing good about a fallen tree.

The trees that stand, however, are the smaller ones, even when their roots do not reach as far as some other trees. In some ways, it is a shame to lose the big trees instead of the small ones, because the big trees have so much history. These older trees have been around for so much, climbed by so many, and yet they are the first ones to fall. God help my friend should his favorite tree be felled by the wind, as he will justifiably mourn that loss.

Those large trees were not always so large. Each tree that is felled by a windstorm was once a smaller tree, bending with the wind thirty or fifty or one-hundred years prior, as the older trees fell across yards and roofs. This is how nature works: that which is old was once young. There is no *static* in nature. There is only change.

The church, in its infinite wisdom, has apparently decided that nature is not good enough, and that change is not something the church should be seeking. Who needs new leaders, when the old ones are so strong and tall, and with such strong roots!

It is true that the church is a conservative institution; this is part of its fundamental nature, as the church seeks to conserve the story of Jesus and the traditions of the early Christians. But this fact of the church's conservatism does not mean that the church is not to engage new ideas and new people. There is nothing in the Bible about shutting off debate. Nor is there anything in the Bible about doing things in only one way. Neither Jesus nor the apostles ever said, "But we have always done it this way!" Instead, the prophet Isaiah proclaims, "Behold, I am doing a new thing!"

Sometimes, the church does its best to dress itself up so that it looks like it is doing a new thing, without living with the risk that actually comes with something new. "We'll set up a praise and worship service to bring in the young people," someone says. It is discussed in committee for hours, and then someone puts something together, and it is either successful or not, but at no point has anyone thought to actually talk to the young people that the church is trying to reach. It is as if the church has forgotten that its mission is to conserve Jesus, rather than the church's understanding of its own importance: as if praise songs written in the mid-1970s will entice twenty-year-olds to want to join the church. Why, I heard of an eighty-two year old man who stood up at his denomination's annual meeting and gave a twenty-minute lecture on how to entice young people to enter the clergy, without having asked one single young person about what to say! This is not the church doing a new thing. This is the church doing an old thing and calling it a new thing.

Meanwhile, the church is top-heavy and in danger of falling. This is what happens when you rely only on the tall trees with the strong roots. Oh, I do not mean that the leaders of the church should just sit down, but you just cannot do sustainable ministry with the same old folks all the time. Eventually—it happens to everyone—the same old folks get set in their ways, and unless there is someone to spur those folks in a new direction, the church will die, and there will be no one to take over. And not only will there be no one to take over, there will be no one to convince the same old folks that the church is on life support. It is clear that we need to bring more folks into the pews, but the extent of the damage cannot be seen, because there is no one on the outside to survey it. The church itself ends up a tall, strong tree, unable to bend and very top heavy. You know what that means.

There is another way.

The apostles were burned out: busy all the time and unable to see to the most basic act of Christian charity. The widows were not getting their food, and people were understandably complaining. There was simply too much to be done, and not enough time in the day to do it all. The consequences of inaction were unbearable: the new web of the Christian family was quite fragile and not yet seriously tested. Not only would the widows continue to go unfed, but the Hellenists would continue to complain about the Hebrews, and the new Christian family would break apart. Schism is perhaps the biggest threat to new religion. The stakes were high.

There were two choices, as there always are: change, or do not change. Though the consequences would have been disastrous, it probably seemed tempting to continue doing things the way they had always been done. There were twelve leaders, and that should have been enough. The arrangement had worked for so well for them. There had been a few nights in prison, but nobody had been killed; they had all escaped harm. Twelve was the number that Jesus had given them, too, and it was important enough that they held an election to replace Judas. Matthias might have wondered why they went to so much trouble to add him to the group, only to pull in seven more leaders alongside him so soon after his election. Too many cooks spoil the soup, you know, so adding seven more leaders to the mix probably did not seem like the most appetizing proposition. Staying the course was probably a temptation.

But staying the course would have been a disaster. The widows would have gone hungry, the Hellenists would have split from the Hebrews, and (though the power of Jesus was still in them) the new Christian movement would have split in two directions. Who knows how far down the road they would have made it. Unity was key, and rather than stick to what they had known, the apostles and all the rest of the bunch did something that the church has forgotten how to do: they changed.

The choice must have seemed scary. So much was changing around them, and the new church was the only thing over which they had any control. Giving up that control amounted to a driver taking her hands off the wheel. This is not often a good idea.

They changed anyway, adding seven leaders to see to it that the widows were fed, and giving up an important part of their ministry to a new group of leaders in order that God be better served in the process.

You know what? It worked. The church changed, and it worked. The widows were fed, and Stephen, one of the seven, did signs and wonders unlike any seen before. It was scary, and fraught with peril, but it worked. The church should take note of this. Change can happen.

## Questions for reflection:

1. How do you need to change? What is one thing you can give up? One thing you can take on?

2. Change is difficult, and it does not mean we should give up our core values just because it would be easier to change. What should be non-negotiable for the church? What could the church change in order to be even more faithful to the Gospel of Jesus Christ?

# Peace
Acts 7

*Lord, do not hold this sin against them.*

All college students know that when taking a particularly difficult exam, there is one last-resort strategy for answering a question about which the student knows nothing: ignore the question and competently answer another one. Some days, I think this strategy got me through seminary, and on the surface, Stephen employs this same strategy in his lengthy speech in Acts 7.

The high priest asks Stephen, "Are these things so? Are the accusations leveled against you by the false witnesses brought to testify against you true? Did you blaspheme God and the temple?"

Stephen ignores this question. It is not that he does not know the answer. He knows the answer. Blasphemy is in the eye of the beholder, after all.

But rather than answer the trumped-up charges against him—what is the use?—Stephen goes into a lengthy excursus on the history of God's people, as if this would satisfy the blood-hungry crowd.

Sometimes, the answer is bigger than the question. Stephen knows that answering the question is a waste of time, so he uses the little time he does left to set the religious authorities straight. Just some advice: if you have the chance to be a pivotal figure in Christian history, you do not want to waste the opportunity.

Still, the question to which I keep returning is this: what gives Stephen the ability to be arrested—apparently for the first time—and respond to these charges with such clarity? Surely, Stephen was scared. Surely, he knew that such provocation would only lead him down the path to death. What gives Stephen such power?

It can only be the peace of God. Stephen, it seems, has the peace of a man who knows himself and knows his God. This peace is what gives Stephen power.

Now, "peace" is a word that gets thrown around a lot, such that it does not even mean all that much anymore. My goodness, when a professional basketball player changes his name to Metta World Peace, I fear that peace has, in fact, become a joke. What does world peace entail, anyway? Surely we can agree that world peace involves no wars. In some ways, the threat of physical violence is just as bad as violence itself, so it ought not be too controversial to say that nuclear disarmament is involved somehow in this grand scheme.

But what about bar fights? Does world peace mean that after a bender, no one will throw an errant punch?

It is silly, of course, but if we are to achieve world peace, we must ask ourselves just what it is for which we are working. Instead, when we talk about world peace, we tend to become so convinced that it will never happen that we abandon the idea altogether as some idealistic goal which is to be embraced only by the idiots and the hippies (and the NBA players, I suppose).

Or, worse, we separate the peace of God from peace in the world, saying that while we can have one, we can never have the other. Why even try?

The problem is that peace is peace is peace, and if one part of creation is upended, all of creation is upended. It is as Martin Luther King Jr. said of injustice: "Injustice anywhere is a threat to justice everywhere." Separating the peace of God from peace in the world just does not make any sense; we cannot compartmentalize the peace of God so that it is saved from the ravages of war and injustice. God needs no protecting. God has an important role to play in the world, and we cannot separate God's peace from the world's peace.

And yet, Stephen has the peace of God that gives him power when the entire world is against him. It is this peace that allows him to see straight through the clouds and everything else and glimpse Heaven: it is this peace that pierces the world and obliterates that which stands between us and God. Stephen's is a powerful peace, and in the face of great injustice, his is a peace given by God.

Unfortunately, this dichotomy is one with which we all must live: we are called to have the peace of God in a world which is in constant tumult. This is a tension of which we are all well aware. Our Sunday mornings are peaceful enough, once we get breakfast made, the children dressed, the pants ironed, the waffle scraped off the ceiling, the dog pulled out of the dishwasher, and the car out of the garage in time to hear the last of the church announcements. Even on that day, we know that worship may be peaceful, but once the service is over, there are a million things to do and a million places to go and wars rage and children die.

Peace? There is no time for peace.

But God calls us to peace all the same, and when Stephen faces the stones, God is there. Stephen quite literally faces the fact that injustice exists; this injustice will beat and bruise him until he can no longer breathe. Still, he has a powerful peace.

This is a foreign concept, you know: peace as power. Gandhi and King may have used this idea, but we convince ourselves that only exceptional people are able to live this way, and besides, they were killed. We can rationalize all we want, and the truth is that few of us will face such large challenges, but the fact remains that there is power in peace. There is resolve in knowing that (as a pastor friend says) "the God who creates us redeems us and sustains us." Even though wars rage, God sustains us. There is powerful peace in this statement, because we will probably never see a day in which the world calms down. We will probably never see an end to bloodshed, and though it is sometimes hard to believe that God sustains us, we must remember that there is power in peace which transcends even the power of bombs and guns. There is power in peace which transcends stones, no matter how hard they are thrown.

Peace as power is a foreign concept to us, but it is truth. The example of Christ is such that we know that death has been defeated, and this is the message of the cross. Even when the forces of death have their way with you, and you hang like yesterday's laundry, then you will see the face of God. There is nothing more powerful than this peace, because it is this peace which sustains us even in times of great suffering. It is this peace which makes us know that God is with us.

Of course, peace is not this easy. We can talk about peace all we want, but when the chips are down, and we are scraping our fingernails against the rock trying to find a hand hold, peace is the last thing on our mind. There is too much to do. We have no time for peace.

This time—this busy time, this scratching, hurried, panicked time—this is the time for peace. Peace in the good times is of no use. We need peace in the valleys. This is what God offers us: when the claws of violence and time and suffering grab us, God will be with us. Nothing more, nothing less. When pain so fills our throats that we can do nothing but let it escape out our mouths, God will be with us. This is God's peace. Nothing more, nothing less, but it is enough.

## Questions for reflection:

1. Why do you think peace is so hard for us to talk about?

2. How should the church speak of peace? How should we work for it?

# Not Magical. Powerful.
Acts 8

*May your silver perish with you!*

Of the cringe-worthy things I have heard from my fellow Christians, among the worst is this: "Well, I have so much on my plate during the week, I just want church to be a nice way to relax. I want to be recharged."

You know, as if you go to church to get your Jesus for the week, and by the time next Sunday rolls around, your Jesus-meter will have run down to the point where you need some more, so you go to church again.

If this sounds ridiculous, consider that this is how most American churches work, more or less. We have this idea that Christianity is a magical religion: that by believing in Jesus, God magically sends us to Heaven when we die, or that God magically makes things happen that would not have otherwise, if only we pray.

But magic has nothing to do with Christianity, except to serve as a counter. Magic, after all, exists for itself. There is no point when David Copperfield makes a train car disappear. There is no greater social commentary going on. There is only illusion. This is the reason, naturally, that magicians have taken to calling themselves illusionists, though I am not sure why this name is any better than "magician." However it is called, magic is about tricks, about drawing attention to itself, about entertainment.

Christianity, properly lived, does not draw such attention to itself, at least not as its main purpose. Christianity does not exist just for attention's sake. The matter is bigger than drawing attention to itself. But try telling this to the leadership of many of today's churches, where the congregation comes to relax and enjoy the show.

I certainly do not mean to indict churches with lively worship. There is nothing wrong with lively worship; the church is expanding worldwide in places with lively worship, and far be it from me to criticize the work of the Holy Spirit. But there is a difference between lively worship and a show, although plenty of churches who put on a show try to pretend that they are doing lively worship. Nobody wants to admit that they are putting on a show, after all, because then they are admitting that the action is all on stage, rather in the congregation where it belongs, and where is God in that? No, nobody wants to admit that they are putting on a show.

Boiled down to its essence, when a church puts on a show, it is magic they are after, because there is no life-changing going on. When church becomes all about filling the seats (with little consideration for much else), the Gospel becomes magic.

*Come this week and fill your Jesus-meter. Come next week when you run out. Keep coming back to this place, because we will make sure to keep you sustained.* The church starts to believe that it can do the sustaining, rather than letting God take care of it.

Oh, churches make excuses like, "We are here to draw people in. Let other churches worry about growing disciples." But the folks who come for the show stay for the show and do not go any deeper in their faith. Why should they? This is all about magic, and I can get my fill right here. Why go deeper, when all I need is being fed to me from the stage?

To this mindset, Acts 8 gives a resounding rebuttal. To those who say, "We must do whatever we can, advertise however we can, water down the message however we can, spend whatever we must to get people into the church," the apostle Peter says, "May your silver perish with you, because you thought you could obtain God's gift with money!"

Now, really, all Simon the Magician wants to do is heal people with the Holy Spirit, and is this not a good thing? Surely, we can agree that healing is a good thing. So who cares how it happens? Who cares what the means are, as long as the end is justified? And the end is good. No one denies that healing is good.

Peter says, "No." No, you cannot pay us for this power. The means matter. Religion is not just about the end-sum. Religion is not only about the result, the means be damned. No, religion is about something greater than this, something greater than magic. The means matter. Perhaps the means matter more than the end, although this is probably a pretty controversial statement. We are so concerned in the Christian church with whether someone has been saved that we forget that the saving act of Jesus Christ happens to all of us, all the time, and God's grace is not something you can own, no matter how much healing you plan to do and no matter how much money you plan on giving to the capital campaign. In the United Methodist Church, we talk about going on to perfection, and I like this idea. The grace of Jesus Christ is continually working within us, taking us to new heights of Christian expression and spurring us on to deeper Christian living.

Too often, the church has taken this powerful and life-changing witness and turned it into a magic show. Watch now as I take a rabbit out of my hat! I will now saw this woman in half! And, abracadabra, the tomb is empty! Isn't that nice? See you next week.

Contrast the modern magic show with the way the Gospel really works.

A eunuch is reading scripture, and the apostle Philip runs up and immediately starts talking. That Peter is running is nothing remarkable; I imagine you have to run fairly fast to catch up with a chariot. What is remarkable is that Philip talks to the eunuch—and not only this, but Philip gets into the chariot and *sits down*. Perhaps such an act does not sound unusual, but in Philip's day, this was simply not done. You do not fraternize with the help, especially when said help is understood to be a sexual deviant. Customs exist for a reason, and you do not just go around breaking custom willy-nilly.

Philip gets into the chariot anyway and reads scripture with the eunuch, helping the eunuch to understand its meaning and grow into a disciple. It is interesting that this conversion involves working to understand scripture—hard work, after all—rather than the eunuch coming immediately to believe. Philip does nothing showy; he does not demand a conversion, nor does he heal the eunuch's man-made wounds. There is no physical restoration. The eunuch remains a eunuch, and culture remains culture, so the eunuch will continue to be marginalized by society. There is no easy road ahead for this eunuch, and life will be made all the more difficult by this particular choice of religion, for the choice will only lead to more marginalizing, more potential for persecution. If this is healing, I am not sure that I want to be healed.

The healing is more subtle than a physical healing, but it is no less powerful. The eunuch solicits help in understanding scripture, Philip instructs, and the eunuch grows in the faith. Rather than asking for an appointment to be baptized, the eunuch spies a river and asks Philip, "What is to prevent me from being baptized?"

Well, so much prevented the eunuch from being baptized. The metaphor is not perfect, but this would be like the modern church baptizing a tree. Why waste the water? So much existed to prevent the eunuch from being baptized, and thus these kinds of religious ceremonies were simply not done. For one, the eunuch was seen as a sexual deviant, and these are the kind of people who were not seen as deserving rites like baptism. The law declared them unclean, anyhow, so Philip—an upstanding Jew, at least until right about now—had no business sitting with him in the same chariot. You can almost hear the bystanders complaining about the two sitting side-by-side. *Oh, how people will talk about this one!*

What is to prevent the eunuch from being baptized? So much, but for all of the reasons, none of them are too much for God. There is no social stigma, no lot in life, no painful childhood tragedy that is too powerful for God. There are consequences to earthly events, and the eunuch will forever bear the scars of childhood trauma, but none of this is too powerful for God.

So we hear an Ethiopian eunuch, scarred and stigmatized, rejoicing all the way back to Ethiopia. If you listen closely enough, you will hear the rejoicing still. Given the choice between the eunuch and the magician, I choose the eunuch.

## Questions for reflection:

1. The saying goes, "God works in mysterious ways." How do you understand the ways in which God works in the world? How are the ways in which God works different from the ways we wish God would work?

2. What is keeping you from accepting God's power in your own life? What is keeping the church from doing the same? Why do you think we would rather view the church as somewhere to get recharged rather than as a place where God does powerful things?

LESSONS FOR TODAY'S DISCIPLES

# The Courage of Ananias
Acts 9

*So Ananias went and entered the house.*

You have probably never heard the story in Acts 9 referred to as "The Courage of Ananias." In every Bible I can find, the story is called "The Conversion of Saul," and that title is all right, I suppose. Technically, it is true: Saul, through a series of signs from God, is converted. This is a wonderful story, and I do not mean to take away from the drama of the moment, so allow me to start from the beginning.

The story of Saul's conversion is a terribly dramatic one. If the story of Acts were a movie, this would be a high point, for sure, with dramatic music and the booming voice of God, before the cameras cut to a close-up of Saul's amazed and anguished face, as he realizes that he can no longer see. Because of this drama, we know that this story is quite important in the narrative of Acts, even if we do not yet know the rest of the story. Imagine those hearing the story for the first time, sitting on the edge of their seats, waiting to hear what happens next.

This is quite a dramatic story, and because we are a people who like drama, we tend to ignore the rest of the chapter. How can we be expected to worry with the rest of the story, when we have seen something so dramatic? God in Jesus is surgically interjected into the story, and we become blinded like Saul because what we have seen is so dramatic, so fantastic, that nothing else matters. It is easy to hear this story and take it as a given that Saul will regain his sight and do great things for God, never mind the rest of the chapter. When you have seen the face of God, you become blind to other things, because nothing is as magnificent as the face of God. Everything else pales.

But there is more to the chapter than the conversion of Saul, and so I think that the title, "The Courage of Ananias" fits just right. Were it not for Ananias, Saul would have had a life-changing experience, yes, but he would have remained unable to see, confused about what had happened to him and unable to go out into the community without considerable help, let alone preach the Gospel.

We do not think of the story this way, because the drama is all on Saul, and once Saul is blinded, we need a break from this big drama. This story is so big that we need to rest a while before we travel through the rest of Acts, and we skip over Ananias without too much attention. Of course, God spoke to Ananias just like God spoke to Saul, but the cameras are focused so much on Saul that we miss Ananias. Without Ananias, there would have been no Paul; Saul's story would have ended with his blinding.

Allow me to press a little further, because the church has a tendency to see Paul as a one-man traveling band, an evangelist who needs little more than a mere traveling companion and a bedroll to spread the Gospel and author the very first Christian theology to appear in Scripture. The letters of Paul were written before the Gospels, and were it not for Paul, there would have been little systematic about how we think about Jesus: just four Gospels to compare to one another. Paul is a crucial part of Christian theology, and the church sees him as a superstar—which he is, of course—but the church also sees him as one who is self-sufficient. Paul is so great, the thinking goes, that he needs no one but himself.

Paul needs no help, other than his Damascus Road experience, and look how successful he is, traveling all over the Middle East and

## Lessons for Today's Disciples

Europe making converts. He is the very model of a traveling evangelist, needing nothing but food, water, and the blessing of God. Listen to some churches, and you'd think that Paul, not Jesus, was the messiah.

But without Ananias, there would have been no apostle Paul. And I can think of few better examples of the power of the Gospel than Ananias's decision to heal Saul, despite the stories of persecution, despite the history of Saul's zealous and murderous ways. These days, we execute people like Saul; we do not forgive them.

Yet, Ananias goes anyway. Not immediately, of course, but then he would have been a fool to go immediately. You do not walk into a murderer's lair without thinking things through. Even though it was God doing the talking, Ananias has to work some things out first. "I have heard from many about this man," Ananias protests. "He has the authority to imprison anyone he wants. He has killed my friends."

I would expect God to rebuke Ananias. When Peter questioned Jesus, the response was, "Get behind me, Satan!" rather than a gentle encouragement. These must be special circumstances. After all, it is not a lack of faith that holds Ananias back; it is Saul's violent history. Ananias would be crazy to go straight to Saul without this questioning, all things considered. Far from rebuking, God reassures.

"Go. I have chosen to use Saul to spread the Good News before Gentile and Jew alike. He will suffer for me. You must go."

Now, the optimist in me wants to skip the part about the suffering. I would like to think that Ananias went to Saul for completely pure reasons, and only with the best intentions. But there is something about suffering that makes me believe that Ananias would not have gone without this statement from God. Does Ananias, a believer, wish suffering on another? I do not know. Without this statement from God, however, I doubt that Ananias could have gone. The suffering is something of a mark of authenticity. Rather than Ananias wanting Saul to be hurt, Ananias knows that the cause is so great, and the stakes are so high, that without suffering there can be no true discipleship.

So he goes. Ananias lays hands on Saul and says, "Brother Saul."

Brother Saul. These are words from Ananias, not directly from God, and yet they are truly healing words. Ananias, whose friends and fellow travelers have been imprisoned and killed by the actions of this man, Saul, greets him as a brother.

God is powerful. But until Jesus comes back, there is one thing that Ananias can do that God cannot, and that is greet Saul as a fellow human, as a brother or sister in Christ. Do not take this lightly, for it is a subtle but monumental point. Saul is blind and does not see Ananias enter, but Ananias announces his presence with "Brother Saul," and in those two words, the thickness of the air in the room has been lifted, because Ananias has shared his humanity with Paul.

This kind of radical transformation is impossible without the sharing of humanity, and it is the responsibility of all Christians. Paul was blinded by his experience with God, but he was healed by his experience with Ananias.

This is not to remove God from the situation. God is central to what we do. But until we let God work within our humanity to further the church—until we remember that one of the most profound ways in which God works is through other people—we are all going to end up with scales on our eyes, blind and scared and unable to move.

And so, in some ways, "Brother Saul" is not only one of the bravest statements in the entire Bible, considering Saul's penchant for persecution. It is also one of the Bible's most profoundly theological statements. Within these two words, we see forgiveness, divine power, healing, and the kind of sharing of humanity that is required for wholeness. These are some powerful words. Could you say, "Brother Saul?" I think that I could not.

But that is the power of sharing in humanity. "No man is an island, entire of itself," writes John Donne. No person is an island:

not even Saul. This is the power of sharing in humanity: that by sharing the core of what makes us human, healing will result.

And this is a strange phenomenon, for while clerics and performers alike look for a way to overcome our humanity in some sort of Gnostic search, it is our very humanity that allows us to be in relationship with one another. We forget, for instance, that Jesus was fully human, sharing his humanity with those around him. It is this humanity that connects us to God. Far from looking beyond humanity, Christianity is a religion that looks deep *into* humanity to find healing.

Though he needs some prodding, Ananias understands this interconnectedness. He goes to Saul, calls him "brother," and watches as scales fall from Saul's eyes. The church may see Saul as a lone ranger, but the reality is that no such thing has existed in all of history. It is our humanness that connects us to one another. It is our humanness that connects us to God.

No person is an island. Should we forget this, we might as well have scales on our eyes.

## Questions for reflection:

1. How has God used unexpected people in your life?

2. Much of the church's power is related to its connectedness, and the fact that God made us for one another. Being in connection is difficult work! How might God be calling you to be courageous enough to reach out to others?

LESSONS FOR TODAY'S DISCIPLES

# When the Spirit Moves
Acts 10

*What God has made clean, you must not call profane.*

There are few things more delightful than watching a child walk down an unfamiliar path. Left to her own devices, she will spend most of her time looking down at her feet, hoping to find something unexpected. I have known children to dig for days through newly-laid pebbles on a playground, looking for a fossil or a broken arrowhead or some such treasure. I, myself, was once such a child.

These treasures are not useful, of course. No child I know tries to reconstruct the full arrow in order to take down a buffalo for the family dinner. But the usefulness is secondary, if it is a factor at all. The magic of the find is the thing; the unexpected is what matters. Look down at the grass and hope to find some broken pottery or a busted piece of tile. Tightrope-walk the edge of the ocean in order to find some sea glass or a poor, dried-out sand dollar. Who knows what you will find?

Once we come of age, we trade this ability for other, more useful skills. If we search for seashells at all, it is to put them in a vase in the guest bathroom. We un-learn an important part of what makes us human, and when we come across monumentally unexpected lessons like that which is housed in Acts 10, we note the story, contemplate the characters, and move on to the next chapter.

For just this once, comb through this passage as if it were pebbles on the playground. You will be amazed at what you find.

The chapter starts when Peter, a model Jew if there has ever been one, has a vision in which God lifts the restriction on eating unclean foods. Actually, to be fair, God does not so much allow Peter to eat unclean foods as God tells Peter that there is no such thing as unclean food. If it is food, it is clean.

This change in diet seems small at first, but look more closely at Peter and you will find a man whose life is defined by that which is acceptable and that which is not acceptable. Peter needs no imagination, really, because everything in life has been set out before him. Eat this. Do not eat this. Do this on the eighth day. Do not do these things on the Sabbath day. In return for following these rules, Peter has the knowledge that his are the chosen people, set apart from the rest of humanity and special in the eyes of God. Being the chosen people is worth following some extra rules, after all.

Of course, Peter's vision is about more than simply expanding his palate. His is a profoundly life-shaking vision, and much of what Peter knows about himself and his place in the world dies, in that single moment. The sheet from heaven might as well be a shroud. How can Peter continue living? What is the purpose of rules, if they continue to be broken?

I cannot stress this dilemma enough, though it seems quite small in retrospect. Peter has lost an important part of himself, and it is for his own good, but it is a loss nonetheless. Peter must set out on the important journey of learning how to live once he has moved beyond archaic rules of what to eat and what to avoid. It is much easier to live with the rules, if not a bit dull. But the Holy Spirit has called Peter to move on, and so move on he does.

Only, this is not about food. Oh, in some ways, it is about food, but much more than that, as with most things in the Gospel, it is about people. Were it only about food, Peter would be in less of a tight spot. Do not want to eat shrimp? Do not eat shrimp. It is that easy. But when it is about people, the breaking of the rules is much more difficult, because it comes along with Jesus's teaching to love your neighbor. Vinegar and baking soda are no problem on their own, but combine them, and you have quite a mess. When you must love your neighbor *and* deal with unclean people, the formula for success becomes trickier, because those unclean people are now your neighbors. You know what they say about good fences.

Before Peter has time to process his vision and mourn the loss of part of his religious identity, Cornelius's men yell up to him, calling him down from the roof and his vision. The Spirit tells Peter to go with them, and so he goes, after letting these unclean men spend the night in the same house in which he is staying.

Peter goes with the men, trusting the Spirit. He must trust the Spirit, because there is no telling what awaits him. Is this a trap? Are the Romans going to capture him? Perhaps the religious leaders are tricking him to see if he will, in fact, break the Jewish purity laws. No matter, because Peter goes with the men and enters Cornelius's household, which breaks the rules plenty, thank you very much. But it is what Peter says to Cornelius that changes everything. These are among the most monumental words spoken in all of scripture, and indeed, all of history.

"I truly understand that God shows no partiality."

If the Sanhedrin could hear him now! They would slap the words right out of his mouth, because what Peter has said goes against everything it means to be a Jew.

No partiality? What is left for us, then? Table scraps? Nobody wants the table scraps. Everybody wants to be first in line at the table so that they get the good meat, not the leftover bits. But what Peter says is that God shows no partiality, plain and simple. In every place, in every walk in life, God accepts all those who fear God and do what is right. In the eyes of God, there are no longer "chosen people." There are only "people," and for God, this is enough.

And with these words, Peter throws the doors of the church open to all who dare to enter. There is no checking the driver's license at the door. There is no means test, or literacy test, or theology test. Peter has opened the church to all who fear God and do what is right.

This is good, of course, and the only problem is that Peter has taken the rules and broken them into a million pieces. The rules exist for a reason, and not only has Peter broken them, but because the rules are in scripture, he is acting contrary to scripture! Some rule bending I can take, but I draw the line at flagrant abuse of scriptural commandments!

In all seriousness, this is quite a dilemma for the follower of God. On the one hand, we have the primacy of scripture: scripture is the primary means through which we experience and understand God. On the other hand, we have the Holy Spirit, who seems utterly unconcerned about what Leviticus and Deuteronomy have to say about unclean food.

Things were much simpler before the Holy Spirit got involved. We did not have to worry about where we were going, because the map was given to us, in detail, and all we had to do was follow the directions. And for all the good that has been done by Peter's throwing open the church doors—including, by the way, allowing *this* Gentile to be a Christian—the way ahead is full of potholes and road hazards. What this means—what the Holy Spirit's involvement really means—is that anything can happen. *Anything* can happen.

As if the Christian life were not difficult enough already, now we have the unknown variable of the Holy Spirit that could show up at any moment and rearrange the puzzle, such that all we can do is figure out a new way to make everything fit.

If this concept does not rattle the very core of your being, you are much stronger than me. This is scary, the idea that there are directions which may no longer apply. The apostles lived with this possibility every day, but two thousand years later, things have calmed down. We are back to Newton's second law the theory of relativity and one plus one equals two. We get frustrated when the trains run five minutes late. We expect what we expect, and when things do not work out as planned, we panic.

# Lessons for Today's Disciples

The work of the Holy Spirit is scary, because there is no number on the Richter scale for the fluctuations we feel under our feet. If we cannot rely upon Leviticus, on what can we rely? Suddenly, it is much harder to be a Christian than to not, because the Christian life is about so much more than following the rules. The Christian life is about following God, about listening to the Holy Spirit. Living up to these high expectations is a very audacious goal. It was hard enough when we just had to follow the rules. Now, God is asking us to look beyond them. Losing these guardrails is scary, but God calls us to take off down the road anyhow. As Jesus said (in so many words), it is the law of love that most matters.

God does not simply push us down the hill without a guide. For as scary as following the Holy Spirit can be, God does offer one constant. The Holy Spirit moves in only one direction, and that direction is love. If it is of God, if it is of Holy Spirit, it is of love. This is not to throw out scripture, by any means, but neither is it to ignore the work of the Holy Spirit who sometimes works contrary to the rules.

Most days, I think that blindly following the rules would be much easier than living the adventure of faith that comes through following Christ. Perhaps this is true.

I have found, however, that the adventure of faith is so much more rewarding than it is easy. It is difficult to re-learn that child-like sense of wonder, that creative spark that is driven less by law and more by love; the world has taught us so much to the contrary.

Yes, it is difficult to follow in the adventure of faith, but in the final analysis, there is nothing more delightful than remembering how to walk down an unfamiliar path, picking up things as you go along. There is nothing more rewarding than following the living God who is full of surprises.

See what the work of love has done. Cornelius and his entire household receive the Holy Spirit and extol the goodness of God. Peter opens his heart to an entirely new group of people. The church expands beyond Israel and beyond the life of all the apostles, such that all people, in all places, in all times, are invited to learn of the goodness of God. When the Spirit moves, you lose some certainty. But you gain so much more.

## Questions for reflection:

1. Think about a time in your life when simple rules were not enough. How did you deal with the anxiety of being set free?

2. Freedom is much more difficult than bondage. What are some ways in which God calls us to be free?

# Lessons for Today's Disciples

# In the Face of Tragedy
Acts 11

*Now those who were scattered because of the persecution that took place over Stephen traveled as far as Phoenicia, Cyprus, and Antioch.*

In ascending order, I have heard the most foolishness come from the mouths of the following people: politicians pandering in a debate, tipsy college students after one too many, and ministers presiding at a funeral.

I wish I were exaggerating, but I am afraid that I believe this to be quite true. I once heard a minister at a funeral trying to explain—explain!—the death of a child, as if the death of a child were perfectly explainable: as if it would all make sense if only everyone in the audience understood. Foolishness. As one poet has said, the only proper response to learning of the death of a child is to roll over and play dead.

When tragedy strikes, there can be no explanation that suffices. We understand the physical nature of death. The body shuts down and ceases to function, and we die. But there is just no explaining death itself in a way that satisfies all our curiosity, hope, and fears surrounding the event. Even when the death is expected, after a life well lived, the mystery remains. There is no simple explanation that is good enough. I was in college when my grandfather died in his eighties after a long illness. The day he died, I spoke with a professor about his death, letting her know that I would be absent while at his funeral. And you know what she said to me? She said, "Well, it's the circle of life" and she went on grading her papers, as if quoting a movie theme song was supposed to make me feel better. Well, no, that explanation did not help. There are no words that suffice. When tragedy strikes, sometimes only the silence can properly speak.

Tragedy is much more than death, of course. There are other tragedies besides death. We are a tragic species, the human race. We lose jobs, friends, limbs, property, and abilities. We are always losing things, but then again, losing things is part and parcel of being human, and tragedy surrounds us all. If you think things are going pretty well for you, just turn on the news and watch what flashes across your screen. What you see will be coming to you, soon enough.

When tragedies do come, we try to explain them away. If we can explain them, we can control them, after all. Just think about science: as humans have begun to understand more and more of the earth and how it works, we have used that knowledge to control the earth to our advantage. We like control, because when you have control, you cannot lose the things that humans lose. In the face of tragedy, then, we like to try and explain away what has happened, if only because the silence becomes too loud to bear.

I am left to wonder what Stephen's family was told after his stoning. Can you imagine the things that the mourners told his family? Just think back to the last funeral you attended, because those are the kinds of things that were said to Stephen's family.

"Oh, I hope it was not too painful." *Well, yes, having rocks thrown at you is painful.*

"He died for something he really believed in." *A lot of good that did him.*

"God must have wanted another angel." *Why could God not wait and let us keep him longer?*

There are just no words for this kind of tragedy, and we do a disservice to try and explain it away, especially when we implicate

God. It is a natural inclination, to bring God into the situation, because God *is* in the situation. Of course God is involved, because God is always involved. I shudder to think of a world in which God is not involved.

But in our haste to include God in these most tragic of moments, we say the simple thing, which is that God must have wanted this tragedy to happen. It must have been that way, we say, because God is in control. Listen to this idea, and picture yourself hearing it as the parent of a child who has died. Perhaps you have lived this scenario.

This explanation is just foolishness. God did not want your child to die. God does not kill children. There is nothing in scripture to back up that idea, any more than there is anything in scripture to back up the idea that God is purple and lives under the sofa. Scripture tells one story, and that story is about the goodness of God, at all times, everywhere. God did not kill Stephen; a group of humans killed Stephen. God does not ordain tragedies.

In his little book, *Markings on the Windowsill*, Ronald J. Greer titles his chapter on tragedy, "Tragedy Makes No Sense," and though that is a trite descriptor, I think it is about right. Tragedy makes no sense. There is no sense in tragedy; do not bother looking for it.

This is a difficult road to hoe, because we are forced to think about God in a new way. When free will enters the equation, and we must bear responsibility for our actions, things become harder, because we have no one to blame but ourselves. God gives us the freedom to do what we want, when we want, and with this freedom comes responsibility. It was much easier when we assumed God controlled every one of our movements like a grand puppeteer.

There is no puppeteer. We are not empty-headed sock puppets, waiting for a divine hand to move our mouths and direct our actions. God does not work this way. And so the great human unknown enters the situation. Tragedies happen because of the unknown. People die: not because God ordains tragedy, but because God gives us freedom.

Maybe we are framing the issue of tragedy in the wrong way, because the word itself has so much finality associated with it. In some ways, there is finality in tragedy, because if a person is not dying, a certain way of life is dying, and everyone knows that death is the capital-e End.

But then again, the great Christian promise is that death is not the end at all, but the beginning of something even greater before. When Paul says that to die is gain, he is not saying that death will be a walk in the park. He is saying that what Jesus promises us is that death is not the end.

God does not ordain tragedies, God sure does have a way of picking up the broken pieces of life and making something new out of them, because look at what has come of Stephen's death. His friends and fellow Christians scattered after his death, because they could not look in the mirror without seeing Stephen's face. Persecution followed them everywhere, and when they were gathered together, they were an easy target. Perhaps they were so broken in their grief that they thought they could escape God. No matter; they scattered.

And look what mosaic was built from the broken pieces of their lives. They traveled far, and if they were trying to escape God, well, God refused to be done with them. The hand of God was with them, and before long, there was a thriving church in Antioch, many miles away. Not even a famine could stop the work of God, and the church in Antioch banded together to make sure that everyone had enough.

Stephen did not die for this. Tragedy makes no sense. But look at the good God has done with what remained. Lives were changed. People were fed. And the church continued on, moving outside of what it knew so that it could encounter all types of new people, including (I might add) you and me.

Still, tragedies continue. Two thousand years later, in Jesus's homeland, the tragedy seems to be constant. Rival religious and ethnic groups fight, constantly, and there is so, so much death. The major world religions are in a blood-war over the very land Jesus called home, and to celebrate his ministry, they fire rockets at each other. As sad as all this destruction and death is for us, it must be completely heartbreaking for God.

In the midst of this tragedy, a Palestinian doctor works to defy that tradition of violence. Though he is a Muslim from Gaza, he frequently treats Jewish patients in Israeli hospitals. You cannot truly stand up against violence until you build relationships with those whom your side considers the enemy. So he treats Jewish patients and occasionally appears on Israeli media.

In late 2008, Israeli armed forces attacked the Gaza strip in response to several rocket attacks from that area. Desperate to communicate with his Israeli friends, and even more desperate to keep his family safe, the doctor maintained regular telephone contact with Israeli journalists. An Israeli tank showed up outside the gate to his home to protect him, and the doctor knew that because of his efforts at building relationships across ethnic and religious lines, he and his family would be safe.

And, as a thanks to the doctor's important work, two days after showing up at his house, the tank fired a rocket straight through the doctor's window, and the shell ripped through the bedroom of three of his daughters. They were killed.

Just like that, in an instant, three of his daughters were killed by the very people who he thought were keeping him safe. There are no words for a tragedy such as this: only silence will do.

If the doctor retreated into himself, quit practicing medicine and spent his days being bitter, you could not blame him. Losing one child is horrible; losing three, at the hands of those you have spent your whole life helping, well, there are no words. There is only silence.

But the doctor did not keep silent; he simply could not. He did not stop practicing. He is a doctor, after all, and healing is what he does. Not healing would have been like not breathing, so he went back to work.

The Israeli government gave the doctor a sum of money for each daughter that was killed: small penance, but a considerable sum. And you know what the doctor did? He took the money, every penny of it, and set up a fund to help Palestinian women and girls. The blood money, coupled with donations from many, many others, is touching the lives of countless girls in Gaza, protecting them, educating them, and teaching them to work against violence.

God does not ordain tragedies. But do not tell me in the face of tragedy, God is absent. There are too many little girls in a school in Gaza for that to be the case.

## Questions for reflection:

1. Think about a time in your life when you had personal tragedy. How did you deal with it? How did others help you cope?

2. Tragedy is all around us, and it can be enough to make you want to close the curtains and never come out again. How do you think God might be calling you to venture out into the world? How do you think you might participate in God's work of grace in the face of tragedy?

# Worms
Acts 12

*He was eaten by worms and died.*

In the United Methodist Church, the liturgy traditionally used for communion goes like something like this. Some other denominations use something similar. The minister says, "Hear the good news: Christ died for us while we were yet sinners. That proves God's love for us."

And while we hear all the time about the good news of the Gospel, since that is technically what "Gospel" means, I like this particular formulation that we use in the communion liturgy, because there is an unstated side of this stated truth. When someone says, "well, the good news is that . . ." we brace ourselves for the bad, even struggling to hear whatever good news is coming first as we wait for what is coming. In the communion liturgy, the minister does not say, "Now, hear the bad news," but the implication is there, and really, the minister need not say anything.

We act out that part of it when we take the bread and the cup. The action of taking the Lord's Supper is bittersweet, as we are remembering—and actually taking part in—the sacrifice of the cross. We are, in some ways, living out the bad news of the gospel.

But you will not hear a minister say, "hear the bad news," because we know that the surprise of the Gospel is that in Jesus's death and resurrection, we find eternal life. This is good news for all of us who believe, even if remembering Jesus's death reminds us of our own.

Remembering your own death can be a painful experience. Most present for me is the humbling notion that I am going to die. Some of us accept this fact better than others, but regardless of how we accept it, we are all going to die. Thankfully, in the Christian church, we acknowledge eternal life. Hear the good news: Christ died for us while we were yet sinners. But the bad news . . .

The bad news is that, as my physician father says, there is just no easy way to die. Oh, death is welcome in many cases, whether it comes after incapacity due to age, or after great pain, or after debilitating illness. We sometimes welcome death as a compassionate force which begins the process of lifting our burdens—God finishes the job—but there is just no easy way to die.

Have you had the privilege of sharing time with a dying person? I have occasionally had this honor, and each time I do, I am presented with two very sharp and very profound realities. The first is that dying is hard work. The breathing becomes heavy, the body seizes, the mouth opens wide in order to take in more air.

The second is that one day, I will be called to the difficult work of dying. One day, my mouth will hang open, my body will seize, and my lungs will struggle to take in air. This may be the most humbling knowledge I know of, because it means that no matter how I excel in life, no matter how much work I put into anything, one day I will no longer be.

I have heard people say that what matters is the dash between the two dates on the gravestone. I do not like trite advice, but perhaps there is some truth in this statement. We are all going to die. You are going to die. I am going to die. It is part of life, this dying.

## Lessons for Today's Disciples

For now, though, we are living. While we live, God calls us to discipleship. Hear the good news. God loves us while we live, and when we die, we go to be with God.

I worry that when we talk about the "dash" being what matters, we ignore the fact of death. That is the point of such advice, I think: do not concern yourself with death. Just enjoy your life for as long as you have. And while this is sound advice in some ways, we must remember that for those of us in the church, God is calling us to the cross. The Gospel is good news, but death is real.

I wonder how James took this news. He knew the risks of following Jesus. If Jesus's own crucifixion were not enough to convince him, James knew that Stephen had died, and so James knew that the possibility of death was there. His work was dangerous. The authorities were after him. It was only a matter of time.

But I imagine that you do not really understand the crucible of death until you are actually experiencing it. This is the problem of death: no one lives to tell about it. Some people "see the light," and some people are clinically dead for a time, but no one truly dies and lives to tell the tale.

I do not know how James accepted the fact of his death. I doubt that he could fully accept it, as he did not completely understand what he was experiencing. But I think that James's continued work in the face of constant threat of imprisonment and death shows that he was ready. He understood his limitations, and he knew that in the face of violent power, there would always be the chance that he would be murdered.

He accepted that he was going to die, and that the Gospel was calling him to the cross, and so that is where he went. Perhaps he did not march straight there with his head held high (we do not know), but he went to the cross nonetheless, knowing that the God who loved him would continue to love him in death, and in a new and fuller way.

If James gives us a good model for following God all the way to the cross, then Herod gives us a chance to see what a disaster denying your own death can be.

Herod wanted nothing of death, you see, and who could blame him? He was king! He was the one with the power, and nobody was going to tell him to die! How could they? Here is a man who lived his life knowing, quite literally, that he—and only he—was above the law, and there was nothing anyone could do to stop him.

It is something of an amazement to me how quickly we forget our own frailty and humanness when we are in power, and Herod was no exception. Herod—known as Agrippa in other non-Biblical writings—spent much of his young adulthood in debt, and it was only through the generosity of family that he was allowed to come out of it. What is more, Agrippa's father was murdered for political reasons when Agrippa was only three years old. Death comes to everyone, sooner or later. No one is above the law of death, king or otherwise.

We forget about the law of death when we have reason to forget it. When power is the issue, it becomes the most important thing, every time. You know the old saying, "Power corrupts. Absolute power corrupts absolutely." Power becomes the most important thing, such that those with it cannot believe in anything but themselves, let alone their own pending deaths.

This is what happened to Herod. Faced with the choice between believing in his own death and believing in his ultimate power, he chose the power, which humans tend to do approximately 100% of the time.

He did not stand up and say, "I will not die," of course. Nobody does that, if they want to be taken seriously. Herod was more subtle, at least in his own mind. So he did two things to show his own invincibility. First, he issued death warrants for the two prison guards who had allowed Peter to escape. With power over another's life and death, how can you not start to think that your own death is negotiable?

Then, to settle a dispute between two nations, he preened himself, stooped so that his assistants could set on his heavy royal garments, and stood triumphant before his people as they waved banners and sang songs praising his name.

"The voice of a god, and not of a mortal!" they sang of their king. He did not correct them. Why would he? In his mind, there was little difference between the two, so there was nothing to correct!

Having rejected his own death, being far too busy and far too important to accept it, he promptly died.

Herod was eaten by worms, which, of course, is what eventually happens to everybody.

Either believe me or do not, but death comes to everyone. Accept the fact of death, and know that God will use you. Perhaps you will not spend so much time trying to avoid the inevitable.

## Questions for reflection:

1. Does knowing of your own death change the way you think about life? Why?

2. Why do you think we spend so much time and energy avoiding death? How can the church be better about embracing death as part of life? How might this change how we live out God's call to be the church?

BECOMING THE CHURCH

# The "E" Word
Acts 13

*Blaspheming, they contradicted what was spoken by Paul.*

I sometimes have the happy occasion to train first-time mission team leaders. People who take mission trips are some of my favorite people, and so I always enjoy our time together. We talk about what to bring (double the money and half the clothes!), how to be culturally sensitive (watch what you do with your hands!), and how to deal with conflict in the team (be the boss!). We talk through logistics, travel health, team selection, and anything else that might help these brave leaders once they step onto the mission field. There is a lot to cover! Mission work is complicated. The training session takes the better part of a day.

For everything else we cover, the thing we inevitably talk about the most is evangelism, and I have learned to block off a good chunk of time for this discussion. The team leaders never bring it up on their own, not really sure how to broach it. But as soon as I say the word "evangelism," it can take us an hour to talk through the issue.

When I first started doing these trainings, I would wonder how adult Christians—many of whom have grown up in the church—could have no idea about how to share their faith. It is not simply that many of us have questions about how to do evangelism in a new culture: it is that we are often unsure how to share our faith, in any culture, including our own. We feel inadequate in the responsibility of bearing the message of Christ.

To put it bluntly: we are excited about mission but petrified of Jesus.

Now, this formulation probably sounds strange to you, and if I am honest, I will admit that it sounds strange to me, too. Nobody should be afraid of Jesus, least of all faithful churchgoers who attend worship twice, three times weekly, and who are now preparing for mission service. But it is true. We are afraid of sharing their faith in places with which we are not familiar. Many of us are afraid of sharing our faith at all.

I should tell you that I totally understand the fear.

There was a time in my life when "evangelism" was a dirty word, and I rejected it completely. You could hardly blame me, with all the awful things I had seen done in the name of the Gospel. Perhaps you have seen some of these tactics, too. I have had more than one person tell me I was going to hell because of this or that belief, but my experience is nothing compared to some of the horrendous ways that Christians "evangelize."

I once read a note from a doctor who had just returned from leading a mission team to a remote part of South America. He and his group were doing great work, inoculating kids against a deadly disease that was completely preventable. All the children needed was a simple medication, and the doctor and his group had plenty. In his note, he said, "We gave out medicine to 327 children, and we received 327 professions of faith."

Well, no. Perhaps the children mouthed the words, but there was no true conversion going on. I do not doubt the power of the Holy Spirit to work in dire situations, but the implication—which might have been stated; I do not know—was that if you wanted to live, if you wanted the medicine that the doctors were waiting to give you, you were going to tell them that you accept Jesus as your personal Lord and Savior, whether you understood what you were saying or not. Just say those words, and the medicine you need to live is yours.

How cruel! This is not the kind of love that we read about in the Gospels. This kind of approach is closer to blackmail than Christian love. The medicine you desperately need is right there, and all you have to do is pledge allegiance to a god that you might not have met before, whom you may know nothing about. Simply agree to upend your entire belief system right then and there, and the medicine is yours.

The aims are good, of course. I have no doubt that the doctor and his group meant well. It is hard to fault them, too, for the life-saving work they were doing. They meant well, but good intentions are not enough.

Take Paul and Barnabas, for example. There was no question that they had been called to the work of evangelism. The Holy Spirit said, "Set apart for me Barnabas and Saul for the work to which I have called them." You just do not get a clearer call than that! Paul and Barnabas went out with the clear blessing of God, and they marched right into the synagogue and waited for their turn to speak. Paul was a well-regarded teacher, at least in the Jewish community, so they let him speak. Much of Acts 13 is comprised of his long sermon.

They had suffered, he said, but God was with them, promising them a savior. Salvation had been a long time coming, and it had finally come in Jesus.

And it went well. Paul and Barnabas shook hands at the door, and the folks in the synagogue raved over the sermon. "Oh, I hope you come back next week," they said, which is what you tell the guest preacher as you exit the church, no matter whether the sermon was good or not. Still, many of them followed Paul and Barnabas, and I am sure that it seemed to Paul that the call from the Holy Spirit was real: that it had not been a dream, that God was doing great things through their ministry.

If Paul was riding high on his sermon the previous week, it was not long before the facts of life brought him back to earth. The very people who had complimented them the previous week, the very ones who followed them, pledging allegiance to their God, well, these people were now denouncing them, contradicting every word they spoke and ruining Paul's hard-fought credibility among the Jews. If this is how you treat me after I offer you the Word of God, never mind altogether!

Paul's experience is a big reason people tend to run screaming from evangelism. Why put the effort into evangelizing—and it can take up a lot of effort to work up the courage—when the possibility exists that we will be shot down completely, run out of town and publicly contradicted by those who we thought were listening? What if they do not listen? So we do things like avoid talking about our faith completely, or requiring—implicitly or explicitly—a conversion in order to receive medicine, ensuring success. Only, I would bet that if you went back to that remote village in South America today and talked to those children who had received that life-changing medicine, you would not find a Christian among them. There was no follow-up after the doctor's visit: no teaching, no discussion, and certainly no relationship. Only a small white pill, a paper drinking cup, and a temporary conversion. If that doctor went back to that village today, I expect that he would be as frustrated as Paul and Barnabas after being run out of the synagogue.

Rather than wallow in their frustration, which is probably what I would have done, Paul and Barnabas turn their focus to the Gentiles, who are quite interested in hearing from them and learning about God. The rest of Acts continues the story of the evangelists' successes in gentile territory, and the gentiles "were glad and praised the word of the Lord."

What Paul and Barnabas learned, and what drives me when I think of evangelism, is a two-fold approach to spreading the Gospel. First, listening to God is key. Paul and Barnabas did not go out without considerable prayer.

Listening only to God in prayer is not enough. You must also listen to God in other people. This was part of the problem in the synagogue, and it was the entire problem in the remote village in

South America. You cannot properly share the Good News without being in relationship with other people. Those children in South America spoke the words of acceptance, but how much good could have been done in the name of the Gospel if that doctor and that team had taken the time to actually build relationships with those kids? How much relationship was missed?

Of course relationship is vital to evangelism. But relationship is a two-way street. I am leery of those who say they are going to another country or culture to "bring Christ to the people." There are so many problems with this statement that I am not quite sure where to begin. If one believes he is "bringing Christ to the people," the implication is that he is unwilling to *find* Christ *in* the people.

Think of it this way. Even if I come to you with the knowledge of the Gospel, which I consider to be the greatest piece of knowledge ever shared among humans, how dare I expect you to simply accept it without my listening to you, my being in relationship with you, my willingness to share in parts of your life as you share in parts of mine?

If I am not willing to share with you, then I am trying to force feed you, and what reason do you have to listen to me?

Share in relationship, however, and entirely new worlds are opened up. If you are willing to listen to me, and I am willing to listen to you, then God is glorified. The theologian Howard Thurman says this: "If I hear the sound of the genuine in me, and you see the genuine in you, I can go down in myself and end up in you."

What a wonderful image! Imagine: evangelism not as proselytism without regard for another's point of view, but as a relationship through which God is glorified.

And here is a bonus: when Paul and Barnabas began to share the Gospel in a way that was open to the needs of others and the will of God, the world was opened to them. I do not know of much news better than that.

## Questions for reflection:

1. Why do you think some people are so scared of evangelism?

2. The world is increasingly multi-religious. How can we be authentically Christian, while still being respectful of others' beliefs? Should we ever change what we believe about God based on what we learn from others? Why or why not?

# On Seeing God
Acts 14

*The gods have come down to us in human form!*

The day had started out well enough for Paul and Barnabas. Driven from city after city, they had settled in Lystra, a city in what is now Turkey. People were finally getting the message there in Lystra, and Paul and Barnabas breathed deep sighs of relief. The pair had finally evaded the religious leaders who had followed them around from town to town, turning crowds against them. The Word of God was being preached, and nothing could stop them.

If their successes had not been enough to encourage them, they also had the healing of the man who could not walk to pick up their spirits. There is just nothing like a healing to put some pep in your step, and Paul and Barnabas were finally starting to shake off the rejection they had received in the synagogue. It looked like lives were being changed, people were being healed, and Paul and Barnabas were being used by God. It is a great feeling to know that you are an instrument of God's love, after all.

Everything was coming up roses until the folks in Lystra had trouble understanding the message of the Gospel after watching Paul and Barnabas heal the man who could not walk. Rather than praising

God for healing the man, they started praising Paul and Barnabas—and calling them the names of their own gods!

"Hermes! Zeus!" they called out to them.

Really, it is understandable, considering what the residents of Lystra had just seen. A man was miraculously healed, and the people called out the names of the gods they knew. You go back to your own experience when something extraordinary happens. On its face, the healing did not make much sense; one does not just get up and walk after a lifetime of immobility. So the people went back to what they knew: that which was most deeply ingrained within them. You need those deeply held beliefs to stand on when things get strange, and stand on their beliefs is exactly what those people did. They knew Zeus and Hermes, and so they assumed that it was Zeus and Hermes who were standing in front of them.

There is a wonderful movie called *Searching for Bobby Fischer* which tells the story of Josh Waitzkin, a young chess prodigy who must deal with his talent as he deals with everything else involved in growing up. Young Josh must decide whether to be himself, and play chess in a more sportsmanlike way, or to be like Bobby Fischer, and take no prisoners. Much is made of the fact that after Fischer won the World Chess Championship, he vanished. No one knew where he was; he simply disappeared.

As Josh grows in his skill, he finds himself wanting to become more and more like Bobby Fischer, despite the chess master's notorious antics. There is a point in the film when Josh, hearing commotion surrounding a chess player in the park, exclaims, "Bobby Fischer!" and runs to the table where the game is being played in order to watch the player generating the commotion.

Fischer is not playing; it is someone else. But Josh is not really looking for Fischer himself. No ten-year-old boy is going to find one of the most wanted men in the world. What Josh sees in that game is something that reminds him of Bobby Fischer, though perhaps "remind" is not a strong enough word. Josh wants desperately to be a grand master, to succeed at the highest levels of chess, and what he sees in that chess game is a reflection of his highest hopes.

When Josh says, "Bobby Fischer!" he is not looking for Bobby Fischer. He is looking for himself, evaluating what he sees and trying to decide whether to become like those players.

All of this is to say that Paul and Barnabas could have worse problems than people believing they are gods. The people hear the commotion surrounding Paul and Barnabas, and so they naturally gravitate towards them, wanting to see what is going on. They watch what is happening, seeing the care with which Paul and Barnabas treat those in need of healing.

I imagine that the bystanders had two thoughts. I imagine that they saw the situation from two different sides; this is how we process things we see as amazing. First, they were simply astonished by the way in which Paul and Barnabas acted. Clearly, these two men knew something they did not, because if the simple fact of the healing were not enough, they were astonished by the fact that these two took the time to heal the man at all. The man listened to them preach, and apropos of nothing, Paul told the man to stand and be healed. Empathy such as Paul's is not an everyday thing. It should be, but it is not. We are surprised when we see such kindness. Such kindness must come from somewhere, hence the naming of Zeus and Hermes.

But there is another, deeper reaction which follows this scene. Even more than being shocked at the kindness of Paul and Barnabas, the bystanders were looking for God.

Forgive me for being cliché, but if we are to talk about God, we must be honest about the deep yearning for the divine that is simply part of being human. Even those people who disavow belief in God often speak of yearning for the divine and mourning that they are unable to find it. Perhaps it is possible to stand outside on a clear night and watch the stars without hoping for a greater order, without desiring God. Perhaps it is possible, but I am unable to look up without feeling that somehow, the deepest root of my humanity is inexorably latched to the most transcendent part of God. At the very least, this is my deepest hope: that the God who set the universe in motion is at work within me.

I am unable to look at the stars without looking for God, and this is how it was with those folks watching Paul and Barnabas. They are looking for God, however they can find God, and here, in this healing—in the gentle kindness of this moment—they have found what they were looking for.

"Zeus! Hermes!"

Well, no, not Zeus and Hermes. Paul and Barnabas. But you understand the confusion. What has just happened was miraculous, and the kindhearted work of these two men pointed straight to God.

In a way, then, the bystanders were right to call the name of God. It was the wrong god, of course, but it was the god they knew, at least until Paul set them straight.

Yes, Paul and Barnabas could have had worse problems than people believing they were gods. The error had to be corrected, naturally, but it was the work of Paul and Barnabas that allowed the light of God to shine through.

This work was just what the bystanders were waiting for. They were looking for God, as they lived out the humdrum of their lives, dealing with everything that comes along with being a human: the sweat, the pain, the wonder. They found God in Paul and Barnabas, even if what they found was different than what they were looking for. The search for the Holy Grail leads not to the cup itself but to the God who drank from it. The calling out of Zeus and Hermes was about the Divine presence within Paul and Barnabas, not the physical presence of a mythological figure.

If we are to find God, we must look within one another, for this is where God lives. What is more, if we are to be true witnesses to the miracle of the Divine, we must live in such a way that others see God within us. Perhaps what they are looking for is not quite what we are offering, but with God's help, the Spirit within us will be enough.

The day had started out well enough for Paul and Barnabas. There was confusion about who they were and what they were doing, but they did not need to worry.

The God who calls out to us from the farthest star was with them, and within them. Show this knowledge to others, and God will never be far away.

## Questions for reflection:

1. Have you seen God at work in others? Where?

2. How might God use you in order that others may see God?

BECOMING THE CHURCH

# Church Business
Acts 15

*The apostles and the elders met together to consider this matter.*

The excommunicated Roman Catholic theologian Alfred Loisy is quoted as saying, "Jesus came preaching the Kingdom, and what arrived was the Church." I do not know what made him say this—I would bet that it was his excommunication that made him say it—but for me, there is no point at which I more aware of this dichotomy than when I am in the midst of a large group of people conducting church business.

I know that it is necessary, this church business, and it is all part of ministry. Ministry is not just about visiting the sick and preaching and wearing fancy robes. There is a certain mystique to what pastors do, since most people only see their pastor once a week, but the mystique is not just limited to pastors. People tend to think that being a Christian is just about being with people and singing hymns, but for every hospital visit and every dollar tithed, there is a report to complete, a denominational audit to review, a mailing to go out.

So I am most aware of the difference between the Kingdom and the Church when I am doing what we call church business, which really just boils down to all of the ministry that nobody wants to do. We tend to put off this work as long as possible and do it all in one big stretch, so that if we are going to be miserable, we might as well all be miserable together, and get it all done at once.

If you think folding mailers is like pulling teeth, just try your hand at hammering out matters of doctrine and theology, an experience more like pulling teeth without anesthetic (or, for that matter, a dental degree). As in, it is painful *and* messy.

We just cannot seem to get along in the church. Oh, we usually manage all right Sunday to Sunday, but get a big group of Christians together and it seems like nobody can agree on much of anything. It is little surprise that we argue so vigorously about divisive issues like abortion and homosexuality, but we could do a better job of being civil about it. And just about everybody has ended up on one side or another of the argument about what color to paint the narthex. With so many different kinds of folks in the church, we just cannot seem to agree on anything.

We cannot help but argue. These are life-and-death-and-beyond decisions we are making. In some ways, absolutely nothing is more important than deep matters of faith. A little passion is warranted, at least in most cases; I am not so sure that I care what color the narthex is painted, but I do care about how the church's mission budget is spent, and what the qualifications are for church membership. These are not inconsequential matters.

I may get just a little heated in my defense of that which I believe to be vital ministry. Hopefully I will not offend anyone, but if it happens, so be it. I am standing up for God.

A little bit of passion is good, but before long, we are all standing on our chairs yelling at one another. I do not need to tell you how ineffective this kind of conferencing is. Neither is it a faithful way of doing church business, although heated church arguments are hardly new.

Certain teachers were coming from Judea, telling all the Gentile converts that unless the men among them endured circumcision, they would not be welcomed into the Kingdom of God. First of all, these new teachers directly contradicted Paul, and he did not react well to those who would contradict his teaching. This instinct has not changed in two thousand years of Christian history: try challenging the pastor's authority and see what happens.

If contradicting Paul were not enough, there was also the practical issue of adding to the burden of the converts: as if risking life and limb for the sake of the Gospel were not good enough, now they needed elective surgery! The street corner prophets who hold signs proclaiming the wrath of God and the need to repent would have to add a line to their posters. We would also need a new line in our morning worship announcements in church, explaining the procedure for becoming a Christian.

Welcome to the church! We are so happy to have you here today. Please feel free to walk to the altar at the end of the service if you would like to become a member. Oh, and you'll need to cut off part of your genitals.

You see the problem.

Certain teachers were arguing this point, however, and so all the apostles, all the leading followers of Jesus gathered in Jerusalem, sort of their denominational headquarters in those days. Luke says that there had been "sharp dispute and debate" between Paul and those certain teachers, which is a nice way of saying that they were standing on their chairs yelling at one another. Things were turning ugly quick, thanks to the passion of both sides, and it was time to come together and hammer out some doctrine.

It started innocently enough. I do not know if they distributed the requisite written reports to all the delegates beforehand, but they started by talking about the great work God had been doing. Everybody knows to start the meeting on a feel-good note, so that people feel like they really are doing ministry, even if it involves debating and voting. You delay the inevitable a bit. You let everybody feel good about things before the real controversy begins.

It did not take long for things to get heated. To the good news of God's work, one of the Pharisees rose and rebutted, "The Gentiles must be circumcised."

And you could have heard a pin drop. Everybody knew that they were gathered to discuss this very issue, and it should have been no surprise, but even when you know what is coming, controversy always brings with it an element of surprise. How do you respond to that which you know is coming? It is harder, in some ways, than speaking off the cuff: all that time to prepare, and here it is, and you can barely open your mouth.

I know of a denominational meeting a few years ago at which the controversial issue of homosexuality was discussed. Everybody knew the debate was coming, naturally. They had been sent glossy fliers in the mail from all sides of the issue. Reporters were calling to poll them on their support of the matter. There were protests outside the convention hall doors. This was no surprise.

And in the tussle over the issue, a communion chalice was broken. How do you respond to a broken chalice?

The delegates at that meeting knew that the conflict was coming, but nothing could prepare them for what happened when the issue actually came up.

Those gathered in Jerusalem also faced a difficult meeting. The issue was not really about circumcision. It was about circumcision in some ways, I suppose, but it was only about circumcision in the way that the argument about the color of the narthex is about the color of the narthex. There was much below the surface, many hostilities to be dealt with, and the issue was more about "who gets in" than the particular religious ritual that garners Luke's attention.

Peter, who has had his own dealings with the Gentiles and who God left in charge, does not take the bait of the provocateurs. God has given the gift of the Holy Spirit to the Gentiles, he says, and the only thing that separates the Jews from the Gentiles is a small patch of skin that only half the population is born with, anyhow. Does God truly care about this small patch of skin so much that the Gentiles must undergo a painful operation in order to be welcomed into the church?

There is no name-calling, no standing on the chairs, no broken chalice. Peter, Paul, and the rest of the bunch talk about all that God is doing, and in the end, they compromise. The Gentile converts will not be forced to undergo circumcision, but certain ritual laws remain:

no meat from strangled animals, no sexual immorality, and no food offered to idols.

So much at stake, and they compromised. They figured out how to include the greatest number of people in the Kingdom, and they budged on the rest.

Imagine that. The fate of the church and of the world decided in a meeting. It was church business, after all.

## Questions for reflection:

1. Those of us in the church often decry the politics involved in institutional life. Those outside the church often cite the same politics as a reason that they remain outside the church's walls. How might we frame church business differently, so that God may be seen and experienced within it?

2. In the interest of making everyone comfortable, we often separate church business from the rest of the life of the church. Could we do church business and meetings differently in order to better do justice to God's grace? What might such a change look like?

Lessons for Today's Disciples

# God's Justice
Acts 16

*Do not harm yourself, for we are all here.*

The prison scene in Acts 16 is just so ridiculous that I do not know where to begin discussing it.

I do not mean to suggest that the Bible is ridiculous, or that Acts is ridiculous. But Acts 16 shows Paul and Silas acting in such a strange way that most of the chapter just reads like a joke.

Paul and Silas are arrested for casting a demon out of a slave. They are stripped, beaten, and thrown in jail. That night, while they sing hymns, an earthquake throws open the prison doors and unshackles the prisoners. Rather than running away from those who wish to kill them, Paul and Silas stay right where they are. They visit the jailer's home for a meal and return to the jail in order to be locked up again. After they return to prison, Paul and Silas are ordered released by the magistrates, but they do not go! Only when the magistrates show up at the jail do Paul and Silas finally leave.

If this sequence of events makes no sense to you, do not worry, because it just fundamentally makes no sense. What kind of person would pass up the chance to escape from prison, and then do it again, and then do it again? I hesitate to put labels on Paul, but "bullheaded" comes to mind. It is as if Paul is saying, "If you want me to move, you are going to have to make me!"

There is no time for childish games! There was a lot at stake, after all. There were other evangelists, I suppose, preaching and healing all over the region, but Paul's work was vital. There was so much more work to do, and the new church needed Paul out of prison, preaching and teaching and making converts and helping to grow the church. Instead, Paul decided to stay in prison and put all his chips on the hope that the jailer would not kill him. There were so many others in need of the kind of help and healing that only Paul could provide, and like a fool, he went back to jail, on purpose.

No sane person goes to jail on purpose, particularly when going to jail means the probability of torture and death. Ex-convicts always seem to say, "I do not want to go back there" when they are released from prison. Sometimes they do go back, but certainly not because they want to. Just about nobody goes to jail on purpose.

Except Paul. And Silas. What is more, it seems as though they are ignoring a sign from God and letting a perfectly good natural disaster pass them by. They have been singing hymns in order to calm their spirits. I sing hymns when I need to calm down, so I get that. I will often find myself whistling a tune during the parts of my day with the roughest grit. It insulates you, and it connects you with God. So far, it seems, Paul and Silas are acting perfectly normal.

And just in the middle of a hymn, the earthquake comes. There are few things in life that I imagine sound more like the voice of God than an earthquake, and you would think that Paul and Silas would understand what was going on.

Only, survival does not seem to be on Paul and Silas's radar; at least, survival is not their main priority. For Paul and Silas, the most important thing is the Gospel. And in this case, survival and furthering the Gospel involve opposite tactics, and they choose the Gospel above survival.

There are two parts of this story that make absolutely no sense to me. First is the fact that they so easily overcome what amounts to their own biology—the hard-wired instinct to run or fight when the body is under stress. I think surviving prison, bondage, and an earthquake qualify as stressful situations, and I am left to wonder how Paul and Silas overcame the natural instinct to fight for their survival or to run for the hills. Our brains are tailor-made to initiate this instinct in these kinds of situations, and Paul and Silas overcome the instinct three times running.

The second part of this story that makes no sense to me is that, in many ways, Paul and Silas seem to be disobeying God. God did not tell them to run for the hills, exactly, but it is hard to interpret the earthquake any other way, particularly when you are in the thick of it. If I were in a similar situation—or just a difficult situation that seemed to have no means of escape—and God gave me a clear "out," well, let's just say I would not spend time worrying about what the jailer did to himself. I would pay attention to that which God was doing and come to the obvious conclusion: run!

These two confounding parts of the story are not unrelated. Paul and Silas do not overcome the fight-or-flight instinct on their own; few things are more powerful than natural human instincts, but God is one of them. And truly listening to God involves more than just accepting the easy answer. If Paul and Silas had been looking for a sign, of course, they would have found it in the earthquake. But rather than accepting the answer that would have most quickly gotten them out of harm's way, they listened for the true meaning: the meaning that matched up with the aims of the Gospel, not the aims of their own need for self-preservation. They understood that following God involves recognizing that something much bigger than looking out for yourself, something much deeper than focusing only on the immediate.

In a word, Paul and Silas were concerned with God's justice.

When we as Christians see beyond ourselves and our own need for comfort and self-preservation, and when we truly listen for God's voice, rather than simply looking for an excuse to high-tail it out of a difficult situation, we can be confident that God's justice is being done. When Paul and Silas risk life and limb to change the enemy, rather than simply defeating the enemy, it is God's justice that spurs them to action.

Justice, of course, is a funny word to apply to the lot of Paul and Silas. Justice, in our contemporary speech, is about law and order: making sure that the law is followed, that punishments are carried out. And this concept of justice looks much different, depending on whose side you are on. The jailer probably thought justice was done when Paul and Silas were captured and imprisoned, but that was not the case at all. They were being held quite unjustly, and from this side of history, it is not difficult to see the struggle between Christianity and persecution.

But God's justice has nothing to do with simply following the law. In fact, if the life of Jesus is any example, God's justice is often about breaking the law, and about breaking human convention. God's justice is about listening deeply for the voice of God and not allowing God to be equated with being an upright citizen, more concerned with the letter of the law than the spirit of justice.

If working for God's justice instead of human "justice" sounds too unrealistic, too pie-in-the-sky to actually work in real life, take heart. If the story of Paul and Silas in prison teaches us anything, it is that God's sense of justice is not only bigger than our own: it is also more effective.

In hindsight, it makes so much sense. Imagine, for instance, that Paul and Silas had taken the first opportunity to escape, the first train for the hills. Yes, they would have gotten away. Yes, they would have lived to preach another day. The jailer would have died, of course, and even if he had not attempted suicide, he would have been executed for dereliction of duty.

The simple fact of saving the jailer's life would have been enough, but there was a more political aspect to Paul and Silas's obstinacy. If they had run, the jailer would have never experienced the sacrificial love of Christ. His household would have never been baptized. And the magistrates! Paul and Silas were being held for the simple fact the magistrates would rather exploit a poor, demonized woman for money than allow her to go free. The magistrates would never have been embarrassed by Paul and Silas's deep faith in God.

Viewed in retrospect, it all makes so much sense. Remember this when your sense of justice and God's sense of justice collide. God's justice wins, every single time.

## Questions for reflection:

1. How is your understanding of justice different than God's understanding of justice?

2. The "justice system" is an example of a human understanding of justice. If the church is called to be about the work of God's justice, are there specific ways the church can work for reform of the justice system? How might you be a participant in this work?

BECOMING THE CHURCH

LESSONS FOR TODAY'S DISCIPLES

# The Importance of the Mind
Acts 17

*I see how extremely religious you are in every way.*

There is a temptation, in the life of faith, to admit that true faith is ineffable, incapable of being properly described, and to stop there. "You either get it or you don't," as the saying goes, and there is nothing that can be said to adequately explain it. Words just take away from the majesty of God, and surely accepting faith is enough; we do not need to pontificate upon it in order to receive it. Faith is something beyond words, so why bother?

I understand this temptation. In fact, for me, Acts 17 is a hard chapter on which to write, because I have been to Athens. I have stood on the Areopagus, and I have prayed at the spot where the Athenians worshiped at the monument to the unknown God. I have been to these places, and I feel a connection to them, so it is hard for me to use the finite tools of language to delve into this chapter; it all just feels like too much. What I feel for these places, and for this story, cannot be expressed in words. Trying feels like a fool's errand.

I understand the temptation, because I feel it myself, and there are times in my life when I hear a theological point discussed to death, or when I hear the name of God used to justify some unspeakable evil, or when I simply do not have language big enough for God, that I want to give up words altogether. I want to give up the intellectual altogether and let God just *be* within me.

It is much easier to let the language—and the theology, which after all is just language about God—slough off until there is nothing left but my heart and God's, because in my most honest moments, this is what I desire: to be left alone with God. I want to ignore that which causes me to stumble, or that which I deem to be foolishness, and just be left alone with God.

And while I hope that God does honor this wish in eternity, in the meantime, the sentiment is all wrong. Though I may be tempted to eschew the theological side of God for the tactile, personal side of God, God cannot be bifurcated in this way. You ignore part of God at the peril of the rest of God, because God calls us to be Christians with our entire beings, minds included, and ignoring the more intellectual side of faith because it seems too difficult or because we would rather focus on the emotional side means that we are ignoring part of God.

I may not be immune from the lure of this kind of solely-emotional faith, but I take comfort in the fact that I am not the only one who is tempted to ignore the theological, intellectual part of God. The church as an institution feels this temptation stronger than any. Though I sometimes feel as if there are warring factions within myself, I know for a fact that in the church, just about nobody can agree about just about anything. It is far easier to just be quiet and acknowledge God's presence, and let that be that.

There is nothing wrong with being quiet and acknowledging God's presence; really, you should try it some time.

The problem comes when we leave it there: when using words becomes so tough that we just quit, happy enough to worship the unknown God rather than to think through complicated matters of God and life and faith. The church is the biggest offender, and ideology has little to do with it. Whether the church deems all heady theology to be liberal garbage, or whether the church just wants to water down the concept of God until everybody can get behind it without much thought, the end result is the same.

*The reasonable dies.* We are left with emotion alone, and while emotion is part of faith—vital, in fact—emotion kept unchecked is no way to worship God. Emotion without reason is blind allegiance, and I have to believe that God desires more than blind allegiance.

Besides, some of the most vapid foolishness comes out of our mouths when we stop using our minds.

As easy as it can be to forego the use of our minds in the life of faith, it was even easier for the haughty philosophers who held court on the Areopagus, because when you stand above all others, when you look out and see all of Athens from that perch high above the city, you cannot help but be struck with the majesty of it all.

The theologian Friedrich Schleiermacher talked about religion as fundamentally mystical: as beyond language and therefore ineffable. Stand on a hillside looking over the world and you will see what he means. The feeling you get—the feeling of absolute dependence, of wonder—is maddeningly inexplicable. Describe it, and it will fall apart like clods of dirt.

I do not believe Paul would begrudge me this notion. I do not think you can go through life following God through prisons and earthquakes and hostile crowds without having some deep-seated feeling of faith that defies explanation.

Still, Paul does not stop at this wordless feeling. Paul does not say, "I have faith, and that is enough." Paul argues, engages, and wrestles with God and with scripture throughout all his letters, and he certainly engages the Stoics and the Epicureans and the rest of the philosophizing bunch on the Areopagus in Athens.

What is interesting to me is that Paul does not begin his speech by dismissing the gods of Athens. The temple to the Unknown God did not stand alone; it was the complement to twelve temples of known gods. The Unknown God was a placeholder for any gods who had not yet been revealed to the Athenians, and you can start to see where Paul is coming from when he declares the Unknown God known in Jesus.

Paul tells them that he has seen their altar to the Unknown God, and rather than accusing the philosophers of navel-gazing, rather than disrupting their assembly and proclaiming them all damned, he tells them that this unknown God is known in Jesus. For Paul, the wordless feelings of God and the reasonable understandings of God are part of the same package, and you need both. Accepting the love of God does not preclude wrestling with God in your life and in your mind.

What I see implied in the life of Paul—and what I read explicitly in the writings of Schleiermacher—is a willingness to accept that while much of the life of faith is deep-in-the-gut and unspeakable, we must speak anyway. For his part, Schleiermacher saw faith and theology as a tree: history is the trunk, practice is the branches, and philosophy is the root system. Yes, religion is ineffable at its core, but there is no situation in which faith and reason battle so violently that reason must be discarded. Discarding reason leaves faith untested: stale and brittle and easily cracked.

This kind of engagement with reason—and the United Methodist in me adds that we must also engage with scripture, experience, and tradition—has at its core the belief that God is strong enough to participate in the wrestling match. In order to truly love God with all my heart, and all my soul, and all my *mind*, I must trust that God can stand up to my reasoning.

We as the church have for so long assumed that God is strong enough to stand up to our questions that we have forgotten to make sure that we actually believe it is true. Frame the issue as a straightforward question about God's omnipotence, and you will get a near-universal affirmation: of course God can stand up to our questions.

But frame the question another way, and you will get a far different answer. Should we question God? What do we do with the myriad of contradictions we experience in the Bible and in the world? What do we do when science and religion seem to collide?

Ask the question that way, and watch the church clam up, or worse, throw you out.

I am with Paul. I trust that God is big enough to accept my questions. Why, this just might be an issue of grace: we offer God our paltry questions, our pithy tropes and inadequate models, and God keeps on giving us life and breath and all things.

I have to believe that the most engaged life of faith—the faith that most resembles God's great hopes for us—has this kind of critical thinking at its core. Loving God with all your mind requires no less.

## Questions for reflection:

1. How can you further explore your own faith by questioning what you believe and asking God for guidance?

2. The church is sometimes scared of those who step outside of the bounds of acceptable conversation and dare to ask difficult questions about who God is and whom God calls us to be. Who are some people in your own life who have asked difficult questions that have inspired you to go deeper in your own walk with Christ?

# You Don't Graduate from Church
Acts 18

*They took him aside and explained the Way of God to him more accurately.*

You could load massive landfills with the words that have been spent trying to explain why young adults do not come to church. Most of the theories have come from people well past any age that could be considered young adult, but I understand the worry. There is a measurable lack of young adults in the church, and the problem is real, and people are right to work to figure out just *why* young adults just are not taking to church like generations past.

Forgive this addition to that landfill of words, but one obvious reason the church is having trouble connecting with young adults is that church is a huge commitment! I find myself hesitant to schedule lunch next week, let alone schedule every Sunday morning for the rest of my life. I do not mean to infer that young adults are incapable of committing. But I have been conditioned by the notion that in all I do, I am supposed to buckle down, work hard, rely on myself, and one day, if I am lucky, I will graduate from life. Everything culminates in some completion, I have been taught, if only you work hard enough—school, career, life crises, work projects—and this is how I view life.

Of course, this view of life is entirely bogus; you don't graduate from life. Oh, if you are wed to this notion, I suppose you can stretch it and make it fit: of course the Christian life culminates in glorious completion, but even then I am not sure the metaphor works if we truly believe that salvation is a gift. You do not earn that ultimate graduation, so in that sense it is no graduation at all.

In that salvation is a gift—and so is life itself for that matter—there is a necessary relationship between giver and receiver, and you ignore the giver at your own peril. Church is the natural next step, recognizing that we need others, too, just like we need God. Stripped of its unnecessary vanities, the church is about relationship, after all: relationship to God, relationship to one another, relationship to God *through* one another. And relationship is not something from which you graduate; you do not work hard to graduate from needing relationships so that one day you can throw a party celebrating the fact that you no longer need other people. Who would you invite?

Here is the dichotomy: I have been taught to rely on myself for success, and the church is fundamentally about life-long relationship. You can have one or the other, but you cannot have both, and it seems to me that among the young adult crowd at large, it is the self-reliance that is winning.

Actually, I am not quite being fair. Self-reliance is one thing, but the very least the church could do would be to offer a little guidance, just in case some poor, misguided young adult somewhere decides to, you know, actually try the church on for size. Imagine: the church recognizing that it *is* quite a commitment if you take it seriously and promising to walk alongside young adults, rather than give them prescriptive programming to "get them in the doors."

Instead, you get these old white guys telling us how to bring young adults into the church.

Do not get me wrong. I have nothing against old white guys: I hope to become one someday. But unless we address this issue of self-reliance head-on, we will never get anywhere. It is easy to blame the non-churchgoing young adults for, well, not going to church. What is more difficult is acknowledging that until the church takes relationship—its fundamental purpose—seriously, and I mean *seriously*, nothing will change.

Where did we get the idea that people would be interested in joining up with something that required so much of their time, so much of their energy and passion and *being*, and that they would do so on their own, without any effort from those on the inside? Even college fraternities know that you cannot rest on your laurels, assuming everyone will just flock to you because you are so wonderful!

Recruitment takes work, and not just for recruitment's sake. What I want to ask those people who come up with these great plans for getting young adults into the church is this: what then? What do you do with the young adults once you have brought them in? The church is putting the cart before the horse, and before they try to get more young adults in the pews, they should figure out why young people would want to join the church in the first place.

Until we realize that church takes work, and until we collective agree to spend time with and mentor every single person who walks through the double doors, then church itself is a lost cause.

Church takes work, and you do not get released from work just because you joined long ago. You do not graduate from church; you keep working and worshipping and mentoring, no matter the circumstances.

Priscilla and Aquila had every reason to rest on their laurels. Paul had trusted them so much that he came to live with them, and they had certainly endured hardship, fleeing to Greece from Rome under threat of persecution. The couple was like the church member who says she has served her time, thank you very much, and you can ask somebody else to serve, because I have been there for five pastors and since before they built the sanctuary thirty years ago. Priscilla and Aquila had every right to pass off the responsibility of being leaders in the faith to somebody else. Besides, they were just tentmakers with no special theological training. What made them so special that they could not retire from church duty?

In other words, they could have retired from church work and wondered aloud about why the young adults were not coming to church.

Who could blame them? Not only had they put in their time, but now they were up against Apollos, who was loudly proclaiming an incomplete message. Apollos knew about Jesus, but only as he related to John's baptism. He knew nothing, for instance, of the Holy Spirit. Aquila and Priscilla could therefore have been forgiven for not wanting to deal with him, this loud preacher of incomplete doctrines and half-understood truths.

Let me interject here and make note that mentoring is a two-way street. If Apollos had simply rejected Priscilla and Aquila's advice, he probably would have never made it into Acts. Priscilla and Aquila could have been the most generous, giving, open, caring people in the church, and it would not have mattered. Apollos would have stubbornly gone on teaching the incomplete Gospel, offering incomplete comfort to an incomplete people.

Apollos was open, though, and Priscilla and Aquila were prepared to enter into relationship with him. There is much left unsaid in scripture, but read between the lines and it is fairly obvious that mentoring Apollos was tough work. They had to teach him all that had happened since John's baptism—a lot, after all—and there was work to be done, letting the other believers know that Apollos was the real deal, and he should be listened to and welcomed with open arms. That kind of convincing takes time and energy, and it does not happen overnight.

Church is work—holy work, but work nonetheless—and if we are not willing to work, together, then all we are doing so talking past each other. One of the hardest parts about being a Christian is that while church is hard work, you do not get to retire if you are to remain faithful. We must work, no matter how much work we have already put in, because God calls us to be in relationship with one another. If we are to continue the two-thousand-year-old string of relationships that connect us wholly and directly to Jesus, we are going to have to get to work.

Ours is not a work without reward, however. The time spent with Apollos was multiplied many times in the work he did himself; Luke finishes this little story with an epilogue that justifies all the work that has been done by Priscilla and Aquila.

Apollos crosses over to Achaia, and though he must have been tired from the journey, he remembers the encouragement he received from those who had already put in their time. Luke says—and in his letters, Paul confirms—that Apollos encourages a new generation.

That is what we need. Not ham-handed speeches about the problems of the new generation, and not never-ending discussion about how to get young people in the door. We just need a little relationship work, and that two-millennium connection to Jesus will continue.

## Questions for reflection:

1. The life of faith is about following Jesus and loving other people. This work is never completed. What are some ways in which you (in your present circumstances) can more deeply follow Christ and love your neighbor?

2. One of the fundamental aspects of the Christian life is that it is lived in relationship with others. Think about someone whom you respect. How might you learn from that person? Is there someone you might mentor who could learn something from you?

# Planting Seeds
Acts 19

*So the word of the Lord grew mightily and prevailed.*

If there were any doubt about the power of the Gospel to make people mad, the riot in Acts 19 should erase it. Without so much as a direct word, Paul manages to so enrage the silversmiths who make their money from fashioning replicas of the Temple of Artemis that they whip the entire city of Ephesus into a frenzy. Making these small, silver idols was their bread and butter, and if their work were not hard enough, now this Paul character is coming along threatening their business—and the honor of their goddess!

It is easy to put down these silversmiths, and their tactics were certainly dishonorable, but surely we can at least sympathize with the anger they feel. The trade they knew which brought them great honor (and which was responsible for feeding their families) was under attack. Theirs was a business concern, they said, and since anything goes in business, their anger at Paul quickly turned into full-out chaos.

What is fascinating to me about this scene is that Paul is not directly involved in any of it; he wants to go into the crowd, but the disciples hold him back and some of his powerful friends warn him against it. And because Paul is not directly involved in this dispute, it is obvious that it is actually not Paul at whom the Ephesians are mad. The Gospel being preached by Paul and by others is powerful enough on its own to threaten the deep-seated financial interests of those who profit from religion. Paul is just the messenger.

It must have been frustrating for the silversmiths to see their way of life threatened, but the whole situation just goes to show you what happens when you start messing with people's livelihoods: their true motivations come out. Feel free to try and find some high-minded argument in the Ephesian mob; you will fail. As often happens, they come together in order to get angry, rather than coming together *because* they are angry. Luke writes that the crowd was full of confusion, and that most of them had no idea why they were there at all: no idea why they were so angry. But angry they were, and the riot grew closer and closer to the tipping point.

The fact is that you just cannot read Acts 19 without coming to the conclusion that there is nothing noble about Demetrius's complaints. He is not upset with Paul's *beliefs* except as they pertain to interrupting his financial monopoly on religious devotion. Paul's message—indeed, Jesus's message—is that you need not buy expensive silver idols in order to please God. Pleasing God, it turns out, has nothing whatsoever to do with your financial situation, insofar as the place from where you come is concerned. Not only need you not be rich in order to please God, but being rich is actually an impediment!

These are all familiar themes to us in the twenty-first century, though we have figured out how to ignore the ones that are too difficult for us to bear, like selling it all for the poor's sake. But even more than this, when I watch religious television or listen to so many folks put down other manners of faith, I cannot help but wonder if we have missed the real lesson of this chapter altogether. There is no need to engage in this putting down. The Gospel is powerful enough on its own!

Consider: without speaking a word to them, Paul incites a riot so strong that much of the town shows up without any idea why they are there. This is real power: the ability to make people angry without specific cause points to something much deeper. When people are whipped into a frenzy just by the *thought* of you, you can be sure that you are proclaiming something which affects them at the most foundational level, and the foundation is where we in the church aim to touch people, anyway. Maybe, then, success ought to be measured in the number of riots we incite rather than the number of worshippers on a given Sunday!

That is power. There is no need to go about putting down anybody else, if you truly believe in the power of Christ and the church.

But it seems that we have forgotten one of the earliest lessons that each of us learn as children: stand on your own two feet. If what you offer is good enough, there is no need to disparage everyone else. Putting everybody else down just makes you look small, and that can do irreparable damage to that which you hold dear.

Paul gets the power of the Gospel. He plants seeds, rather than pulling weeds, which is good because Jesus has a few things to say about weeds, himself. It turns out you cannot truly pull up weeds without accidentally pulling other plants along with them, and then you have defeated the purpose of pulling the weeds in the first place.

Paul trusts the power of the Gospel, and though he wants to enter the crowd—I imagine to tell them how ridiculous they are acting, and how their frenzy is not about belief at all—he chooses not to, instead trusting that the Holy Spirit will carry the message forward in spite of the riot, and in many ways because of it.

Look at it the other way, and the contrast is even clearer. Say you are reading Acts 19 for the first time, and that you have no knowledge about Paul's message or about the worshippers at the temple of Artemis. Based on this one exchange, what impresses you the most? Is it the artisans, their transparent financial concerns, and the riot-with-no-actual-purpose? Or is it Paul?

Paul's tactics are to rely on the power of the Gospel on its own, and his success underscores his focus. When he is up against a potentially violent crowd, he lets them go about their business. And when he encounters misguided believers, as he does in the first part of Acts 19, he gently explains to them the redemption that is found in Jesus, and he invites the Holy Spirit to come and be with them.

Can you picture a television evangelist getting these results? I cannot. I simply cannot imagine a modern-day, conflict-loving television personality entering into loving conversation with those who are slightly misguided about the message of John's baptism. More often, we see harsh words and declarations that misguided belief is of the devil, words which do nothing but make that misguided believer defensive, at which point the whole conversation is lost.

What is more, I cannot imagine a modern-day televangelist following Paul's example at the riot in Ephesus, because our religious leaders seem to have a hard time letting the power of the Gospel do its work without stepping into the frame and making ham-handed statements about the weakness (and evil!) of other systems of belief. Can you imagine one of these leaders ignoring any opportunity to speak to a crowd? Paul sees that the power of the Gospel is message enough for this day, and that he will do damage to that message if he steps in. There is no need for Paul. The message is enough.

This kind of seed-laying faith is not easy, of course. It takes humility and the ability to recognize that the Gospel is bigger than each of us. It takes respect for others' beliefs, such that though we may not agree, we can at least be in relationship long enough to figure out what our motives are: if they are worth taking on, or if we should let them go off in a frenzy. And it takes specific and profound trust that the message of the Gospel is strong enough to stand up to even the most misguided of motives.

This is not to say that we should never engage those who misrepresent the Gospel: there are plenty within our own ranks who play that game. But if God and the Gospel are as powerful as we claim, they can stand on their own.

You can choose see it on the confused faces of the rioters at Ephesus, or you can doubt that the God is powerful enough without our help. You choose.

## Questions for reflection:

1. Sometimes, we get caught up in the crowd and miss the presence of God already among us. When have you been allured by frenzy? How might you better pay attention to the holy already present in your life?

2. It is much easier to dismiss those who disagree with us, but God calls us to more. How might we be in relationship with those with whom we disagree, so that we build up rather than putting down?

BECOMING THE CHURCH

# The Long Story of God
Acts 20

> *In all this I have given you an example that by such work we must support the weak, remembering the words of the Lord Jesus.*

One of the benefits of reading a book of the Bible all the way through is that you start to get a feel for the narrative arc of the story of God. This benefit is especially evident in Acts, and if you want the full effect, read Luke, too, so that you can see how the story moves in a detectable pattern, all the way from the angel's appearance to Zechariah in the temple of God, to Paul's farewell speech in Rome. It is nice to have some narrative cohesion. Too often, we see the Bible as disparate parts or lists of holy sayings, and in truth, the Bible is sometimes each of these things but altogether something else entirely.

Even more than just in Luke's two books, there is an obvious narrative arc in the Bible. The Bible as we have put it together over the centuries starts with Creation and stories of how we came to *be*, and ends with Revelation, which if it does not tell the story of the end of everything, at least launches the people of God into the future, its metaphorical language keeping us from being tied down to past events like lead weights, and reminding us that God is still present and active, even today. Look closely and you will see that the

Bible starts with "In the beginning" and ends with "The grace of the Lord Jesus be with all the saints. Amen."

For all the stories that are told in the onionskin pages of our Bible, it is the larger story of God and humans that is the greatest of them all.

Because the Bible is so long, though, and because we get caught up in our own immediate struggles, we tend to downplay our part in the grand story of God and instead focus on what is happening *now*. After all, if we cannot control the present, at least we can pretend to do so, and so the present becomes the thing we focus on the most. It takes too much work to figure out how we fit into history, so we do not bother.

Let me invite you to step back for a moment and look at history from outside it, as best you can. Thinking about the "earth rise" picture taken from the moon helps me. In the grand scheme of history—particularly in the grand scheme of God's history, which is actually the same thing—the parts each of us play fit into one story.

In a strange way, it is comforting to know that the history of God is bigger than my own history, and I say that it is a strange comfort because the common way of understanding a single life against the entire swath of history is to deem it "small" or "insignificant," and there is little comfort in that kind of formulation. Of course, I do not believe we are either small or insignificant, so I do not think this way of looking at things is particularly helpful. What I find comforting about looking at my life against the whole of history is that this way of thinking takes a lot of pressure off of me. I do not mean that God is letting me off the hook in terms of working to transform the world. Far from it! This kind of transforming work is vital to the Christian life.

But looking at my life against all of history alleviates pressure to fix everything, and thank goodness. I seldom despair as much as when I think about all the world's intractable problems, and can make you feel about two inches tall to think of it all. There are so few of us, up against so much injustice, and you almost want to just throw in the towel and give up altogether.

# Lessons for Today's Disciples

When it seems like nothing will ever change, and when the forces of pain and suffering threaten to overwhelm me, it helps me to think of folks whose story is told in the Bible. For instance, from my twenty-first century reading chair, I know that even though it seems at times in the Gospels that Jesus is done for, the best is yet to come. And I never cease to be encouraged by Paul, who is up against so much more than I am.

In Acts 20, Paul begins his farewell tour. He speaks with many people whom he has loved dearly, letting them know that he will not see them again. The speech he gives to the elders at Ephesus is the only speech he gives in Acts that is directed to Christians, and he has every reason to speak highly of himself. Part of the great story of Acts is the swelling of the Christian movement; what begins with the apostles holed up in the upstairs room, scared and praying for God's presence, culminates in speeches to leaders of established communities of faith. This is the kind of career each of us hopes for, or at least I do. I hope that if I work hard, by the time retirement rolls around, I will see tangible results.

Paul has every right to praise his own work, but Paul knows that the thing he has helped begin is so much bigger than the span of his own life. This is why Paul peppers his speech with references to what he has done and what he expects the Ephesian Christians to do after he leaves: he knows that his work fits into something larger that began in the beginning and will end at the end.

If this idea sounds trite, realize that it is exactly these markers that our story fits into, and it is in accepting our part in God's story that allows us to be the most effective disciples. It is also in this acceptance that we are able to find peace, because the work goes beyond a single lifetime.

In fact, in his saying goodbye, Paul gives an excellent model for sustainable ministry. If each of us is one player in the story of God and God's people, we can start to think about ministry differently. It is not easy to think about ministry in this way, because it is not easy to think of the world going about its business without our help.

When a 7.0 magnitude earthquake hit the impoverished nation of Haiti in January of 2010, I was working for the short-term mission agency of the United Methodist Church. The outpouring of support in the days after the earthquake was just incredible; it does your heart good, in the midst of such heartache, to see a response like that. People just came out of the woodwork to offer money and supplies, and I had hundreds of folks contact me wanting to volunteer.

Telling those folks to wait was hard, for two reasons. First, it was hard to tell good Christian folk who simply want to live out God's call on their lives that they should put that call on hold, or at least find another way to live it out in the meantime. Haiti was not yet ready for volunteers, especially on the level of magnitude we were seeing. We had disaster response staff in Haiti already—some had been there during the quake, and two were killed—and the denomination had sent millions of dollars to help the relief effort. We were in constant communication with the president of the Methodist Church in Haiti, and they were specifically telling us to ask people to wait. Mission teams going to Haiti before they were ready would overwhelm the church and get in the way of the trained relief personnel dealing directly with the disaster. There would come a time when volunteers would be needed, but *immediately* was not that time.

The second reason it was hard telling people to wait was that in many cases, people simply refused to wait. I understand the reaction: you see the devastation on the news night after night, and you feel compelled to do something. Giving money, for these people, was simply not enough. And I sympathize; God calls us to go to the broken places in the world and offer hope and healing. These people wanted to go, *now*, and knowing their passion, it broke my heart to tell them that prayerful waiting was the most faithful witness they could offer.

Well, some people went anyway. They decided that there was no need for church structure, if it was going to get in their way, and they went anyway. Some of these groups were able to do some good, particularly in terms of treating patients. But most of these teams just got in the way, hampering our efforts of bringing supplies and offering real relief to those who needed it most. The roads were so torn up, we knew, that getting around was next to impossible, and yet, people went against our wishes.

Tell me: what is the purpose of dropping everything and flying to Haiti, if the situation would have actually been better *if you had not gone?*

The people who went to Haiti in the days after the earthquake did not seem to have a sense of how they fit into the bigger picture. What mattered, to them, was the immediate sense they had within them that they should go, and the feeling is commendable but it is not enough.

If Paul had made disciples without a plan for what came next—without empowering those disciples for life without him—there is no telling what would have happened to the church. But Paul knew that his was just one role—and important one, but just one—in the story of a God who continues to work, generations and generations after Paul could work no more.

## Questions for reflection:

1. Has taking the long view ever changed your understanding of something important? When?

2. The Christian story began before you were born, and it will go on after you pass away. How does the knowledge of God's long story change the way in which you understand your faith?

# Radical
Acts 21

*They seized Paul and dragged him out of the temple.*

The family who sold their house, bought one half its size, and gave the difference to charity. The skinny kid from Tennessee who gave up his comfortable lifestyle to start an intentional community in inner-city Philadelphia. The famous Catholic priest and writer who picked up and moved to a group home for people with developmental disabilities. And the apostle who went to Jerusalem because the Spirit told him to, even though death was a near certainty.

We know plenty of stories of people who heard the serious call of the Gospel and responded with the kind of all-encompassing devotion that serious calls deserve. If you are a regular churchgoer, you have probably heard these types of stories in sermons every now and again, used as examples of why you should take the Gospel more seriously (whatever that means), but hardly ever used as reasons you should *actually* sell everything you own, or why you ought to quit your job and move to Ecuador and work with indigenous peoples.

Preachers tell these kinds of stories because they are good stories, and good stories make people feel as if the sermon was a good sermon, and good sermons make people feel as if the preacher is a good preacher, and you see where I am going.

But these are real stories, and to turn them into some sort of polemic on anything less than *actually doing likewise* is to rob them of their real power and the agony that went into their enactment. You don't sell half of everything you own without suffering through many sleepless nights, and even if you could explain it how it all felt, it would take far longer than a fifteen-or-twenty-minute sermon.

You cannot really blame the preacher, though. Few of us—preachers included—have the bona fides to actually follow through with that kind of radical obedience, so it is hard for the preacher to tell the story from that angle, because then the sermon cannot be preached from an authentic place.

For all of the problems with the way these stories are told, it is a shame that we do not hear more of them, because if we are to truly take the Bible seriously, we are each called to have our own stories of radical obedience.

Paul heard the call to radical discipleship, and if God does not call each of us to Jerusalem, I am fairly certain that God calls each of us to a place where death lurks like a coyote, ready to strike at any moment. I know this sounds harsh, but the Bible can be harsh. Making peace with death—or, at least, the possibility of death—is part of the Christian life, and a very important part of the Gospel message is that, as Christian writer Frederick Buechner says, the worst thing to ever happen to us will not be the last.

Think of Mother Teresa, for example. She lived her life so surrounded by death that it is a wonder that death did not eat her alive.

Going to those dangerous places—and I mean to speak of danger in both physical and spiritual terms—is part of what it means to follow Jesus. I have to believe that Jesus was being serious when he said that those who want to live authentic Christian lives have to take up their crosses and follow him. This is not easy work, and the only thing that will make things easier is abandoning that call altogether.

# Lessons for Today's Disciples

More bad news: the danger is not the hardest part of taking up your cross. The hardest part is that good, God-fearing Christian people will tell you that you are crazy, and in some ways, they are certainly right. Who gives up a comfortable life and modern health care to move to Sierra Leone and care for malnourished orphans? Surely, you should look after your health and stay in a place that has good health care in case you get hurt or sick. You would be crazy to give up that privilege.

Perhaps this kind of dangerously authentic work is exactly what God is calling you to do, but you will hear many voices—many whom you love and trust—telling you to reevaluate that call.

I hear these contrarian voices all the time, and it does not take a grand act of radical discipleship to ignite the chorus. I have seen many church people fired up about leading an international mission trip to a place like Costa Rica (hardly the paragon of danger), only to be talked down from their vision by other church members who think mission trips are a waste of time, or a waste of money, or an unnecessary luxury for an already financially-strapped church.

Dealing with the naysayers can be the hardest part, because at least radical discipleship comes with the peace associated with knowing that you are following God. Start listening to those who would tell you that your obedience is unnecessary, and you will start to doubt that call of God on your life.

If this contrarian spirit came from people who did not have our best interests in mind, it would be easy to deal with. But those who stand for the status quo, and against radical obedience, usually do legitimately care for us and want the best for us. They often believe God is on their side, too, and it is difficult to argue with someone who believes God is on their side.

The disciples in Tyre who discourage Paul from going on to Jerusalem, for instance, are quite certain that he ought not to go. Verse 4 says that those disciples told Paul "through the Spirit . . . not to go on to Jerusalem" and when the Spirit is involved, you are foolish to ignore its calling.

For Paul, who had experienced the Holy Spirit so profoundly in his ministry, this conversation must have been extremely difficult, and it would not prove to get any easier. After he left Tyre, he went to Ptolemais to visit Philip (who had converted the Ethiopian). There, everyone begged and pleaded with him, telling him what an awful idea it was to continue on to Jerusalem.

Paul must have been miserable. Here he was, standing against the wishes of those he had worked so hard to disciple, turned towards a road that, let us be honest, could lead only to death, trying to make sense of his own call while hearing those whom he loved dispute that call. As if the call to death was not enough, he had to deal with those who loved him and wanted him to see no harm!

This nay-saying is particularly insidious, because after a while it starts to look pretty attractive. We can ignore the protests of those outside the church, but it is the concerns of those inside the church that are particularly difficult to digest. After all, these people loved Paul. They were just looking out for what they thought were his best interests. I am certain he was tempted to honor their protests, to refrain from going on to Jerusalem, and to take his ministry elsewhere.

It is insidious, this tendency to discourage radical obedience, because radical obedience is life-grinding work as it is, and we need little discouragement to keep us from the path to the cross.

Paul would not be swayed; his mission came from God, and he knew that the difficult path was the one to which he was called. "I am ready not only to be bound but even to die in Jerusalem for the name of the Lord Jesus," he says (21:13), and he clearly meant it. It was only days before he found himself in the temple, arrested and beaten to within an inch of his life.

Let this be a reminder that the dangers of truly following God are real.

We ask the question of "What would Jesus do?" so often that it loses its bite, and I have to wonder if we should start asking the question of "What would Paul do?" instead.

It takes courage to ask that question of yourself. I would say that it takes so much courage to follow God the way that Paul followed God that only God can offer the courage. The promise of radical obedience is that if we commit to truly following God, the courage will come. Be brave.

## Questions for reflection:

1. Again and again, society tells us to "keep our hands and arms inside the cart." How might you venture outside the box that the world has carved out for you?

2. When have you been brave? Where did the courage come from? How do you think you could leverage this courage in order to do the work of the Lord?

# You
Acts 22

*I am a Jew, born in Tarsus in Cilicia, but brought up in this city.*

One of my favorite religious exercises involves handing out big pieces of paper to a group of folks and asking each of them to map out the story of each of their lives. Some people draw a timeline. Some people draw pictures. Some people stare blankly at the piece of paper, trying to make sense of the disparate parts of their lives.

Staring is ok, too. It is less the resulting lines on the page that matter, and more the overall project of putting the events of life into some kind of order. Almost invariably, people who participate in this exercise end up finding meaning in the events of their lives that they did not see before. This meaning-making is especially true as it relates to how people perceive God.

It can be difficult, in the moment, to make sense of how God is at work in each of our lives. In the thick of it, of course, we have trouble seeing anything but our immediate surroundings, and this spiritual nearsightedness is understandable. When crisis hits, our senses are heightened, and we easily become overwhelmed by all we see and experience. Perhaps we pray for God's aid and feel some sense of peace, but until we start to look at the story of each of our lives, we miss out on seeing just how God has been at work the whole time.

We each have a part to play in God's story, of course, but it is important to remember that God has a role to play in the story of each of our lives, too. Looking back at our own stories is vital to the life of faith, and pretending to hide in the shadow of the cross, ignoring the self, and not recognizing the particularity of each of our own lives leaves us (at best) confused about who we are and how we relate to God.

Allow me to air some of my generational dirty laundry and admit that I find the famous "Footprints" poem painfully saccharine. The footprints poem talks about a dream in which two sets of footprints are in the sand: the dreamer's, and God's. The dreamer notices that in difficult times, there is one set, and she asks God why God was not with her in the difficult times. God says—and is this not just so sweet?—"in the difficult times, I carried you."

Now, the poem is a gross oversimplification of God's relationship to pain and suffering. But what I do appreciate in the poem is the glance over the shoulder. What I do appreciate is the attempt at making sense of where each of us has been and how God has been there with us.

This kind of meaning-making is not unique to Christians. In fact, all you have to do is listen to an in-depth interview with a celebrity to hear the interviewer trying to tease out some greater life narrative. They tell stories about overcoming adversity or not being taken seriously early in their careers, and the theme that emerges is almost always success in the face of great obstacles. For the self-important lot, it is natural that success is the theme that emerges. We all want to be successful.

Celebrities (thank God) do not have a monopoly on life meaning. We all want our lives to have meaning, and this feeling is natural. Part of being a Christian—indeed, part of being a human—is trying to make sense of life and the world. Without some sort of meaning, we are simply disparate people with disparate experiences, and we might as well be goldfish swimming in a bowl. It is this meaning-making that makes us human.

Meaning-making is a human phenomenon, and it manifests itself in the telling of stories. I like this notion, because it means that when I get together with my old fraternity brothers and spend hours telling story after story—some tragic, some comic—it means that instead of just wasting those hours, we are together deeply engaged in meaning-making, and in sharing in one another's life stories.

This is part of the reason why I find the Bible to be such a powerful ally. Reading about others' stories reminds me of my own and allows me to participate in the lives of people who lived thousands of years ago. When I read about Paul, I participate in his story. I am particularly engaged when he looks back at his own life and makes meaning of it.

As Paul stands under arrest before his accusers, it is the story of his life that he tells. He could offer a point-by-point refutation of the trumped-up charges against him, or he could take the opportunity to make a political point about Roman rule. Either of those responses would be entirely appropriate; indeed, he had made those kinds of responses before.

But this time, Paul tells the story of his life—particularly, his life with God—and in the ordering of the story, we can see Paul not only making sense of his own life (in the face of impending death), but we can also clearly see God at work in Paul's life. Paul says over and over in his speeches and in his letters that his life has importance only as it relates to God's mission, but in his defense before his accusers, Paul shines the spotlight directly on himself: not as an act of self-promotion, but as a deeply spiritual way of admitting that his selfhood is important. Indeed, without selfhood, Paul is nothing. If he is to be a vehicle for God, the only thing he can be is himself.

This is such a unique passage in scripture because even though it has been written by Luke and not Paul, we are able to see some of Paul's own logic. We get some of that logic in his letters, of course, but there is great worth in this speech, as it gets at the things that drive Paul. It is in this speech that we get the clearest picture of

Paul's meaning-making, and so we get the clearest picture of who Paul is.

Running through the entire speech is Paul's assertion that his entire ministry has been defined by his endeavoring to be a loyal Jew and follower of God. He has made mistakes, naturally: he speaks of standing idly by as Stephen was bludgeoned with stones. But since his conversion experience, a major milestone by any measure, Paul has sought to be an obedient disciple of Jesus Christ.

This obedience does not mean that Paul has shed himself entirely; Paul's sometimes bombastic personality shines through in his speech and in his letters. And it is Paul's status as a Roman citizen that he cites when being beaten by the crowds in order to be delivered from further injury.

Paul knows who he is, and he figures the story of his life in such a way as to demonstrate the ways in which he has sought to be a faithful disciple. He does not say, when given the opportunity to defend himself, that his own life does not matter. Far from it! Paul's life matters quite profoundly, and without the specifics offered in Acts, we would have a far less clear picture of how to live the life of faith.

Even more, if Paul did not have a clear sense of who he was and how his life was in relation to God, I would bet that he could not have possibly become the great author of Christian doctrine that he ultimately became. Paul is a person of character, and you do not have character unless you are intentional about being the person God created you to be. You do not live the life God calls us to live without a sense of who you are.

Paul's story helps me remember that for everything else God has called me to be, God has called me first and foremost to be myself. This is not to ignore my particular faults and foibles. But it is also not to be so ashamed of myself that I refuse to stand up and accept that my story is the story of God at work in my life. Paul has skeletons in his closet, and he acknowledges them, but he does not allow them to consume him. It takes a strong sense of self to overcome that kind of past.

Ultimately, until each of us goes down deep inside ourselves, until each of us explores the things in the depths of our souls and rises to the surface with a report of our findings, we cannot be in proper relationship with God. Without a sense of self that recognizes our own part in God's story, we will never see God at work in each of our own stories. Relationship, after all, is a two-way street, and if I do not know who I am, I cannot offer myself wholly to Another.

## Questions for reflection:

1. How does your own story color your faith? What insights from your own life might you offer as a gift to the church?

2. Do you have a strong sense of self? If not, what is keeping you from accepting who you are and working to become more faithful? If you do have such a strong sense, how can you keep your ego in check in order that God may speak through you?

# Resistance is Real
Acts 23

> *The Jews joined in a conspiracy and bound themselves by an oath neither to eat nor drink until they had killed Paul.*

I am not surprised by much. I may be young, but I have been around the block enough times to know that in the life of faith, just about anything can happen.

Two things do tend to surprise me, though, and I do not think I will ever get over them. The first is that I am often surprised by the depth of some people's devotion to the Gospel. When I hear of people devoting themselves to a low-income urban mission, or selling everything they own and moving to Zambia, I cannot help but wonder how it is that the Gospel speaks to them in such powerful terms. We are all reading the same book, after all, and yet we do not all enter the mission field.

The second thing that never ceases to surprise me is the level of nastiness good Christian folk encounter when trying to do Gospel work.

I mean, it is just unparalleled. I have seen pastors who have worked hard to fix troubled churches called "Anti-Christ" and "Satan." I have seen ministers' lives threatened over perceived slights in the pastor's visitation schedule. And I have seen Christian missionaries receive death threats because they discovered others "skimming funds off the top." This stuff happens, and it happens often. Nastiness is par for the course of being a committed Christian.

Part of the reason I am often so surprised by all of this is that it tends to be Christians doing the threatening! The worst part of all of it, to me, is that these people who claim the Christian mantle are absolutely sure that they have God on their side. It is just impossible to argue with people who are sure that God is on their side. There are days when I feel as if more evil than good has been done in God's name, and by people who truly think they are being faithful. It is amazing what you can "turn into" faithful behavior when you start rationalizing your behavior without truly seeking God's will.

Look around, and you will see that it truly is possible to rationalize just about anything. God wants me to have my big house. God would be better served by this church having a different minister. God wants me to have this job. God wants us to kill our enemies. If we do not hear a specific word from God telling us otherwise, we must be doing God's will!

We rationalize so much that at some point, we quit trying. We stop even trying to bring God into the equation and start assuming that everything we do is what God wants. It is much easier to assume that you are faithful, no matter what you do, because discipleship is hard work, and we already have so much hard work in our lives that we want the Gospel to be about making us feel better, giving us what we want, and validating everything we already think about the world.

These are strong forces! Try talking to someone who is certain God is on their side, for good or for ill, and you might as well be talking to a brick wall. What is more: try changing minds, and all bets are off. Folks get very defensive, very quickly.

After all, when you challenge that which lies at the very core of a person, that person will recoil, and for good reason. Just as a foundation shift during an earthquake can bring down the whole house, a foundation shift within a person can cause a similar

## Lessons for Today's Disciples

phenomenon. Because we do not like to be shaken, we get defensive. When you start talking about religion—or when you suggest that maybe we ought to actually be taking the Gospel, you know, *seriously*—that is where you run into trouble. People get awfully upset, and the situation usually does not end well.

So, yes, I am often surprised at the level to which some people go to bring down good Christian folks who are just trying to live the Gospel. I ought not be surprised, but the level of nastiness is often so thick you can barely get through it.

Read Acts 23, and you cannot help but hear the familiar chorus. Paul preaches resurrection of the dead, which in and of itself is not so revolutionary. The Pharisees, many of whom were present for his speech, preach the same thing. It was a fairly controversial idea, but by no means was it Paul's alone, and so this teaching is not what gets Paul in trouble.

It is what comes after acceptance that is so scandalous. It is taking Jesus seriously—including the words about the dangers of wealth and the place of the poor in the Kingdom and the costs of discipleship—that is scandalous. This is the kind of stuff that just might make a bunch of people band together to shut you up.

When you think about it, there really is something scandalous about the Gospel. Jesus was publicly angry. He spent his time with social pariahs. He did not work for a living. He did not have a home. He was not respectful of the powerful. He did not go along with the religious status quo. What is more, the message he preached was totally outside the moral order. Why, you base a political paradigm on the teachings of Jesus, and you'll soon find yourself giving away the whole gross domestic product.

You see how this kind of life creates problems for the authorities, who care less about the good society can do than they do keeping everything stable. If everything is stable, if folks do not get too excited, then they will not see their society for what it is: oppressive, unjust, and totally unequal. They killed Jesus for this message, and Paul takes up where Jesus left off, so that there is a violent plot against Paul is no surprise.

In fact, this kind of life creates problems for me, too, as I try to figure out how to navigate the tricky waters of faith in the context of my real life. I guess I understand the authorities' problems with Jesus in a special way, because I have some of the same problems, and I purport to order my life after Jesus's example! I should not be so quick to judge the authorities, since I seem to share an unwillingness to truly follow Jesus in all of the difficult and painful ways Jesus describes. As my dear friend Judson says of Jesus, "I would never hire that guy to be my financial planner."

The surprise, to me, is not that the authorities are upset. If I take Jesus seriously, I end up upset, too. The surprise is that there is a group, more than forty strong, which is willing to go on a hunger strike until Paul is killed. They so want him to die that they are willing to suffer, to deny themselves food, until he is killed. I may bristle at some of what Jesus is calling me to do, but the group of forty takes things to an entirely new level.

It is fairly easy to understand those who justify taking up arms when people are actively trying to hurt us; we may disagree on the specifics of just war and violence, but at least we can understand the arguments. But what the group of forty is doing is so illogical that it makes the hair stand on the back of my neck. Jesus is not threatening them with anything other than a new way of living that will completely upend the world and shake the very foundation of human relations.

All Jesus is doing is changing everything.

And I guess, when you put it that way, it makes sense, this level of resistance. What Jesus is proposing is so revolutionary, so core-shaking, that it is no wonder that forty angry people band together to keep his message from getting out. When I read the commands of Jesus and the defenses of Paul, I get defensive, and I am a professional minister! I can only imagine what those who are not on the "inside" of the Christian church must think.

It is no wonder that there is violent resistance, but that resistance does not mean that Jesus's words are not to be taken seriously: maybe not always literally, but at least seriously. What Jesus has given us, and what Paul has fleshed out for us, is a way of living that understands that resistance is just what happens when all the oppressive powers of the world are in their last throes.

And though it is hard—and though it means running up against so much resistance that we might not make it out alive—I have to believe, at the end of the day, that this vision of the world that Jesus is offering and that Paul is defending is so crazy that it just might work.

## Questions for reflection:

1. When have you faced resistance in your own life? How did you move beyond that resistance?

2. The church faces resistance in many spheres, not the least of which is with its own people. What kinds of resistance does the church face? What might we, as followers of Jesus, be called to do about this resistance?

# The Consequences of Integrity
Acts 24

*I cheerfully make my defense.*

Nobody seems to pay much attention to Paul's speeches in Acts. His speeches are excluded almost entirely from the lectionary; nothing after Acts 19 appears. Paul's letter get plenty of press, but his speeches barely make a blip on the theological radar.

I understand why the speeches do not get much treatment, since they ostensibly are just permutations of one another: the same speech, slightly tweaked to fit the circumstance. Think of a politician's stump speech, or some pastors' sermons. Paul uses his speeches to recount his travels, or to tell the story of his conversion, or to defend himself against trumped up charges, and Luke has already told us these things. The speeches just tell us what we have already been told, again.

Really, this speech-making could be done a lot more simply, if you ask me. All we need from Luke, who wrote all of this stuff down, is a simple description of the circumstances, a brief summary of Paul's arguments, and we can all be on our merry way. It is as if Luke missed the most basic teaching that all writing students learn: use just enough words, and not one more.

But the speeches do offer something that Luke's earlier storytelling does not. We may know the facts of Paul's defense, but the way he presents those facts tells us something very important about who Paul is. Paul may have his back against the wall, but he maintains the character of someone who knows that God is with him.

The other thing I appreciate about Luke's printing of Paul's speeches is that the speeches often give us something against which to judge what Paul is saying. In Acts 24, for instance, we are presented not only with Paul's speech, but with Tertullus's indictment of Paul before Felix, the governor.

What we know of Felix from sources outside of Acts is not flattering. Ancient historians Josephus and Tacitus both speak of Felix as tyrannical, sexually unrestrained, unable to control his subjects, and more than willing to accept bribes. Felix was no saint, and more than this, he belongs reclined on a couch in a Mel Brooks movie, eating grapes and thoughtlessly ordering executions.

Not only was Felix an awful excuse for a ruler, but everybody knew it. You would be hard-pressed to find someone who, in a moment of honesty, would restrain themselves from telling you exactly what a tyrant Felix was. Nobody, but nobody, cared for Felix.

And yet Tertullus's speech butters up the governor like a piece of toast. "Because of you we have long enjoyed peace," he says to Felix. "Reforms have been made for this people because of your foresight," he says.

Please. If it meant personal gain, Felix would have sold out his own wife; in fact, though there is no reference to this fact in the Book of Acts, Felix did in fact divorce his wife in order to marry a princess with the exact same name. This is not exactly gentlemanly behavior.

Tertullus knew that Felix was a joke: a dangerous joke perhaps, but a joke nonetheless. Rather than state his claim with integrity, though, Tertullus brownnoses, and it appears that Felix is just foolish enough to fall for it. Thanks to the insincere praise, Tertullus is able to convince Felix that Paul is a danger to the status quo, and Felix cares only about the status quo.

Paul, on the other hand, offers no such praise. Instead, he offers an impassioned but straightforward defense of himself. He is no political threat; his religious beliefs should not be objectionable to most of those who are accusing him.

In my mind, the mark of a good argument is that it stands on its own merits. If you need to butter somebody up in order to win the argument, then your argument is probably not good enough.

Not that Tertullus cares if his argument is good enough. He is a lawyer intent on having Paul killed, and he does not care if Paul is guilty or not. Tertullus just wants to win.

I once sat in on arguments for a death penalty appeal before the state supreme court. I was a high school student at the time, and the court had set up some sort of direct-learning program for students to watch trials and have discussions with the attorneys and judges once the trial was over. We crowded into the already-packed courtroom, grabbing seats in the floor or standing against the walls, and watched as two lawyers stated their case before the panel of judges.

I will always remember that day as the day that I gained respect for the legal profession. Respect for lawyers can be hard to come by, after all. God only knows how many "one call—that's all" commercials I have seen for ambulance-chasing, opportunistic attorneys. But the two lawyers in this particular case were different, partly because both were public servants. The lawyer arguing for execution was a prosecutor, and she made far less money than she could have in private practice.

The inmate representing the lawyer was a public defender, since the inmate could not afford a lawyer of his own. Now, public defenders get a bad rap. They tend to get portrayed as either idealistic, and therefore clueless, young lawyers right out of law school, trying to make connections so that they can one day enter a lucrative practice. Or public defenders are portrayed as untalented graduates of some two-bit law school who do not care enough about their work to get a higher paying job.

But the public defender for this particular death penalty case fit neither description. Here was a man, clearly talented, who could have easily found work at a high-paying law firm. Instead, he became a public defender. And, after the trial, when we asked him why he chose to be a public defender, he pointed to the case he had just argued.

"If not me, then who?" he said. "Who will defend a death row inmate?"

The most interesting part of the afternoon, though, came when we asked the two lawyers how they felt about the death penalty. This was a death penalty case, after all, and we were curious about how the personal feelings of the two lawyers impacted their arguments.

The prosecutor spoke first. She supported the death penalty, she said, but the way she said it let me know that while she probably did, in fact, support the death penalty, she found the proceedings to be fundamentally sad. The inmate in question was almost certainly guilty; even as a high school student, I could see the facts clearly pointed to his guilt. The prosecuting attorney knew he was guilty, and that her role was to uphold current law. Even though she seemed certain of her win—perhaps because she seemed certain—there was a certain sadness she conveyed as she spoke of the case. Support the death penalty or not—I do not—surely we can agree that the issue is just fundamentally a sad one. Though she had been able to argue a big case before the state supreme court, and even though she would most definitely win, she was sad. Here was a woman who had integrity.

The public defender spoke next. He did not support the death penalty, he said. In fact, his opposition to the death penalty was a big motivator behind his work as a public defender. If he did not represent those whose life was at stake, who would represent them? He did not want to leave these important cases in the hands of those who were less committed than he. He believed his work was important.

## Lessons for Today's Disciples

Some precocious high school student then asked them how they thought the judges would decide. We would talk directly with the judges later, but they were not in the room at this point.

The two lawyers looked at one another, blinked at the audacity of the question, and waited for the other to speak first. It was the public defender who took the bait.

"I will probably lose," he said, and it was not because of his lack of skill. To my untrained ear he had provided good arguments about the use of the death penalty in this particular case. But it was clear that the facts were not on his side.

What most impressed me about this admission—and about his arguments during the case—was that he never once made any claim that was patently false. Never once did he put aside his integrity for a headline-grabbing win. Instead, he competently cool-headedly laid out his case before the justices, knowing that while the inmate was almost certainly guilty, he was entitled to a fair hearing.

I have no illusions that the defender was famous for his generosity or his care for those on death row. We vilify people who care for death row inmates and we celebrate high-power, high-dollar defense attorneys. This was a man who probably drove a used car, who struggled at times to pay his bills, and who spent sleepless nights overcome with the responsibility of holding inmates' lives in his hands.

In short, he had integrity, and integrity has consequences. It may mean driving a beat-up car, or being despised by your colleagues, or—in the case of Paul—ending up on the wrong side of the law.

After Paul's sincere but straightforward arguments fail to sway Felix, the governor announces that he will postpone judgment until the tribune arrives. Surely, this will be in only a few days, but what Felix truly wants is for Paul to offer him a bribe. After all his troubles, a simple bribe will get Paul out of jail, and he will be able to escape from the ravenous group who want his head.

Only, Paul does not give Felix a bribe. Surely he has access to the money; Paul has followers all over, and all he needs to do is make contact with Lydia, the woman he baptized in Acts 16. She deals in purple dyes and has access to however much money Paul could possibly need.

But Paul does not bribe Felix; to do so, in spite of everything, would be to admit that God is insufficient.

Two years pass. Paul continues to sit in prison, all because he will not milk his network for money, since at its heart, much of this nonsense is about a simple bribe. To follow through with the bribe so would free him from prison, but it would chain his heart.

There are consequences to integrity. Maintaining integrity means that though you live the truth, you will probably get punished for it. The flip side is that if you forgo integrity, the consequences are even worse.

## Questions for reflection:

1. Think about a time in which your integrity and your physical/emotional/financial well-being were at odds. How did you react? If you had it to do over again, would you act differently? Why?

2. True integrity involves being consistent in your values and beliefs throughout all areas of your life. How might the church help others reach this consistency?

# Going It Alone?
Acts 25

*You have appealed to the emperor. To the emperor you will go.*

Perhaps my most vivid memory of being a child involves getting lost in the woods. I had a happy childhood, for the most part, so I find it just fascinating that this insignificant little memory comes to the front of my mind so often. I was in no danger, and the whole episode could not have lasted more than an hour. But still, when I think about the day that I got lost, I can almost smell those woods.

My dad had taken me to visit my great aunt and uncle way out in the country where there was nothing to do but go fishing, and so that is what we did. We drove a few miles to a big lake stocked with bass and catfish, and we got out our poles, and we began to fish.

I love to fish. It relaxes my mind and gives me peace. I could fish all day, were it not for the fact that I sunburn quite easily. But at seven-years-old, or whatever I was, it was next to impossible for me to sit still for five minutes, let along the long hours required for afternoon fishing. I tried to sit still, but sensing that my family was getting frustrated with my restlessness, I lay down my pole and went to explore. My great Aunt Mary was more interested in keeping tabs on me than on shooting the breeze with my dad and great uncle, so she followed me as I explored the banks of the lake and walked towards the woods that surrounded half the lake.

When I got to the edge of the woods, I told my aunt that I was just going to peek inside, see if I could find any lizards or some such nonsense, and that I would be right back. She, being in her seventies at the time, knew better than to try to circumnavigate the rotted-out tree trunks that lay all around the ground, so she sat on a stump and waited for me to come out.

She would wait for a long while. I did not come out. I remember the woods being terribly interesting, and while I still love the woods, I felt as if there were something especially almost mystical about these woods. I waved to her, too far out for to hear my voice, as if to let her know that I was not yet done exploring and that I was going to go farther. The woods followed the banks of the lake, after all, so there was no chance of my getting lost. I would come out at the other end of the woods and finish making my way around the lake. No problem.

Somehow, with all normal clues to guide me, and with the lake constantly on my left, I got turned around. Do not ask me how I got turned around; my sense of direction may be lacking, but I know how to follow around a lake. I was a child, and children get lost.

I suppose the reason that the reason I so often remember this little story is that it involves me being on my own for the first time. I had neither guidance nor supervision, and I did not like the way I felt, alone and without someone to guide me.

It was terrifying, the feeling that there was no one responsible for me, and every time I am faced with one of those life-defining decisions that I must make on my own, I remember this story, because, in many ways, I am still terrified to be alone. After all, humans were not created to go it alone: we were created to rely on one another, to be in a community together, to create society. Going it alone is one of the most unnatural things a human being can possibly do, and yet there are times when I can be surrounded by thousands of people, and yet feel totally alone.

# Lessons for Today's Disciples

Perhaps I so remember the story of being lost and alone as a child because this is a feeling I still feel, even now. Life is full of these times, especially for a young adult starting a career and a family, but I suspect that the feeling does not end there. There are times in the life of every Christian when following God means going it alone, and it can make you feel shortchanged, as if this is not what you signed up for. Everybody wants to be in community—to be accepted by others and loved and cared for—but following God means, well, truly following God, even when no one else stands beside us.

Following God sometimes means going it alone, and we are not helped in this by the mythology that surrounds the notion of "doing the right thing." We are fed this garbage from movies and television shows: do the right thing, and it might be hard, and it might hurt, but in the end, you will emerge victorious and everyone will high-five you as they appreciate the good that you have done, against all odds. Why, you might even get a medal in front of adoring throngs of your peers. This is the kind of nonsense we are fed through popular culture. Do the right thing, and everything will come up roses.

The only problem with this formulation is that it simply does not happen often enough to be of any significance. Doing the right thing often means that just about everybody hangs you out to dry. God does not promise divine retribution against your enemies, though this promise would make following God a lot easier, as it would at least make life seem a little fairer.

So you can imagine how Paul felt, standing alone before Festus and King Agrippa. There is no good contemporary comparison; even murderers get lawyers these day. Here was Paul, alone and on his own, standing in front of men who had the power to have him snuffed out entirely. Everybody and his mother had left Paul behind. Not only had the priests and religious leaders—leaders of his own religion!—spoken against him, but they were secretly planning to ambush and kill him.

Truly, Paul was standing on his own. Each time I read this chapter in Acts, I have to slow down and take in every word; the tension is so thick that it seems to interfere with my ability to picture the scene properly, so I have to read slowly, repeating whole sentences in my head, as I try to imagine what it must have felt like to be Paul in this scene. One reason this chapter is so difficult is that Paul barely makes a direct appearance within it; the events of Acts 25 are so out of Paul's control that it is the political leadership that takes the stage. Paul has nobody, but nobody, on his side.

I wonder what I would have done in Paul's shoes.

Leaving aside the fact that I most likely do not have the guts to end up in Paul's present situation, I am so in awe of Paul's fortitude, which is a word that I think was invented precisely for this situation. Paul waits, and listens, and stands in front of very powerful people. He is outnumbered and outranked, but he prepares to present his case, knowing that though he is alone, *he is never alone.*

Paul could have been the bravest soul in history, and I still do not think he would have been able to stand there without God's help; he was simply up against *too much.* But I ought not to concern myself with this kind of wondering, because God does not leave us. There is no situation, human-made or otherwise, in which God leaves us. Even when it seems as if God is as far away as the farthest star, God is present with us. Even when friends and family turn their backs on us—even when they turn their backs on us for good reason!—God is there.

Now, I do not necessarily think that God is with us *more* when we go it alone than when we are with others. This notion runs counter to how I understand community and how I understand the church. God shows up in our relationships with one another. Finding God in those relationships and loving God through those relationships is a big part of what it means to be the church.

But I do think that when I am forced to go it alone—when it seems as if the world is against me—these are the times when God especially *shows me* God's presence in my life. Just as God is present in the relationships I have with others, God is present in the relationship I have with God. When it seems as if no one is for me, when I must rely upon God just so that I may have someone upon whom to rely, that is when God especially shows me that there is simply no such thing as going it alone.

So Paul stands before the king and the entire hall, with its military tribunes and the prominent people of the city. Paul's courage comes from his knowledge that though the defense was outnumbered, it would never be outranked. He understood God's promise: that in the times when we walk alone, we never walk alone.

## Questions for reflection:

1. Have you ever had to go it alone? How did it feel? Did you face consequences?

2. Going it alone is a lonely endeavor. How might the church reach out to those who feel as if they are all by themselves? What if the church fundamentally disagrees with those persons? How should the church react?

BECOMING THE CHURCH

# Truth to Power
Acts 26

*This man could have been set free if he had not appealed to the emperor.*

There seems to be a prevailing sentiment in much of American Christianity that it is important to have Christian leadership at every level of government. I suppose it makes sense: it is those in power who have the ability to affect change, and so we want the people in power to share our values so that they can help us change the world in ways that match with our deepest-held beliefs.

The problem is that those at the top—whatever political party, whatever popular persuasion—did not get to the top because of their unflinching loyalty to Christian ideals. Maybe this is a surprise to you, but it is not the Gospel itself that helps people rise to the top of the political game. You cannot measure faithfulness to the Gospel by a politician's success.

Politicians make deals. It is simply what they do. You will not find a successful politician, for instance, who cares to deal too deeply with the ideas expressed in Acts 2 about communal property, let alone one who believes the Sermon on the Mount to be a guiding principle for public policy. A politician cares about religious ideals, of course, as long as they do not conflict with his or her political ambitions. This, unfortunately, is the nature of politics.

This is not to condemn politics; politics is simply the system by which we order ourselves, and the church is not immune to political posturing. Politics is part of life, and while there are times when I disagree with the person or party in power, I at least know that there will soon be an election in which my voice will be heard. Politics are a good thing, all in all, and removing religion from politics entirely just does not make too much sense either, if we take our religion seriously and our politics seriously. You can't just pretend that one or the other does not exist. Religious devotion does not end at the voting booth; the curtains and dividers which hide your vote do not hide you from God.

But politics will only get you so far. The problem comes not when our religion informs our politics, but when our religion conflates with our politics: when it becomes difficult to tell the one from the other.

I am always interested to hear politicians use Biblical references to support their various political positions. So often, as we look to the Bible for guidance in how to live our lives, it is actually the case that our faith and our politics butt up against one another rather than working together. It is a testament to the fast-talking ways of our politicians that they are able to bend the Bible to fit their platforms. Of course, you can take just about anything out of context and make it look like it proves your point. Just find a fringe group, pick out one of their more extreme positions, and sit down with your Bible and try to find a verse or two that—taken alone—seem to support that position. It is not hard, and not a bad way to spend an hour or so.

You can prove just about anything using the Bible, and so if we are going to be religious beings and political beings—and, for better or for worse, we are both—then we must move beyond simplistic understandings of how religion and politics interact. You cannot just conflate the two, or simply assume that your deeply-held moral position must be imposed on others. While I may have deep-seated beliefs that I believe everyone should have, I have to be careful about confusing my religion with my politics, because there are plenty of people with deep-seated beliefs that directly contradict my own.

When ministers run for office on explicitly religious platforms, I get awfully nervous. Faith informing politics is one thing, but the aims of faith and politics are as different as night and day.

Who knows what Paul was thinking when he went before the king, in Acts 26, but Paul quickly found out what happens when faith and politics collide. The aim of Christianity, after all, is redemption and transformation. The aim of politics is anything but. In fact, mix faith and politics together and there is often quite an adverse reaction.

A little guidance into Paul's motives would be nice, but it is hard to know Paul's intentions when Luke, the writer of Acts, does not tell us much about what Paul is thinking. Acts 26 is actually not concerned at all with Paul's inner thoughts. Instead, what is important is that Paul faces the king, having bypassed the judgment of the governor, and things do not go so well, if you judge things going well by any traditional sense. If Paul's intention is to save his hide, then his appeal to the king is a complete failure. Paul is not set free by any means—the king does nothing to stop his ultimate death, though he does at least note that Paul is not guilty of anything that should require his death.

The King sees Paul's innocence—or, at least, the king recognizes that Paul need not be killed—but this judgment does not help Paul much, as Paul's decision to go to the king in the first place means he will die. There is faith and there is politics, and the faith position is that, of course Paul is innocent. But the politics position is that stability is the most important thing, and the politics of the situation demand that though Paul is innocent, he must still die. Paul may have the moral victory, but that kind of victory does not help him survive.

Surely Paul knew what he was getting into. Surely, he knew that appealing to the King would not set him free. At the very least, he must have understood the gravity of the situation. But then again,

Paul did not so much confuse the aims of politics and religion as he confounded the political system.

Politics, which is (above all things) subject to the law of self-preservation, says that Paul should have done everything he could to save himself. Christian religion, on the other hand, knows that there are things grander than one life—even a life that was so important in the formation of Christianity—and that the kingdom of God is something far larger than what one person can accomplish. When you start to think of religion in that way, Paul's actions make more sense.

The politicians did not understand Paul's motivations, so his appearing before the king must have made little sense to them. The politicians wanted to survive more than anything, and what a miserable existence that must have been. Looking after number one is no way to live life.

But Paul knew a truth greater than they: there are things far worse than death. This kind of radical behavior can come only when you know who the King is.

## Questions for reflection:

1. Think about someone you know who says the important thing, even when there are consequences. What do you admire about this person? How are you similar? Different?

2. Often, the church does a great job of tending to the needs of the powerful, but it does a poorer job of looking after those who speak truth. How might your church reach out to those who have spoken truth to power and ended up the worse for wear?

# Shackled Leadership
Acts 27

*Unless these men stay in the ship, you cannot be saved.*

The longer I am in ministry, the more often I seem to express the same sentiment: "If I were in charge, everything would be fine." If only I were allowed to do the things I felt necessary, if only I were not constrained by church law and politics, if only people would listen to me, everything would be great. It is a conceited thought, but it is a sentiment I find myself feeling, especially when I feel so passionate about an issue that I am willing to tackle it all by myself, never mind the fact that a leader with no followers is no leader at all.

There is wisdom in not always going it alone, of course. Ideas are tempered in community, sharpened in conversation. There is a reason that we go to church. But there is a difference between going it alone and going along with the whims of the group. There are times in which I feel something deep within, when I am quite certain that God is calling me to something (or, likely, calling the church to something), and I feel constrained by my surroundings. It is enough to make you want to just give up.

This is not merely a church problem. Business, family, and politics: there are constraints in every sphere of life, and there are times in which everyone feels tied down, shackled, unable to move.

## Becoming the Church

This is not to say that everything that holds us down is a bad thing. When we start families, we speak of "settling down," becoming tied to a place and a group of people. The church has even been known to sing "Blessed Be the Tie that Binds" on occasion.

Sometimes, though, the constraints are more palpable, more real. Sometimes, the things that keep us down are more akin to the shackles that Paul must have been wearing on the boat to Rome.

I imagine that being on a rickety ship in a storm at sea is quite a different experience when you are shackled, literally, to the boat. I am one who prefers my feet on dry land, thank you very much, and when I am on a boat in a storm, I am exactly not the picture of calm. Upon stepping onto a boat of any size, I have been known to mentally plan my escape route, even on the sunniest of days.

If I were Paul, shackled to the boat as it was tossed about by the waves at sea, I would have been out of my mind. Being held down on land is bad enough, but if the boat that Paul was riding on were to suddenly sink while he was shackled to it, it would not only be the cargo that would be spending eternity at the bottom of the sea. Here I thought the constraints of church life were tough to live with, but the storm that surrounded Paul's boat was so bad that even the sailors who could abandon ship had given up hope of surviving. They would never walk on dry land again, never see their families, never smell grass or eat fresh meet again.

In the midst of this storm, an angel appears to Paul and utters what I consider to be the five most hilarious words in the entire Bible: "Do not be afraid, Paul." Though the storm rages, though you are being tossed from side to side, though everyone has given up hope, do not be afraid, Paul. You must stand before the emperor. God will keep you and your shipmates safe.

Never mind that it must have been little consolation in the discussion of Paul's safety that he must stand before the emperor. Promising to save Paul for the emperor must have sounded akin to saving a death row inmate from an angry mob so that he might face the electric chair. Paul might have had the promise of immediate safety, but he still faced the confines of his ultimate appearance before the king.

This is the context, though: this is how Paul comes to convince his captors not to abandon ship. Had Paul not been shackled, his voice would not have carried as much weight. Paul's fate was bound up in the fate of the ship, and it was precisely because of his tether to the ship that he was able to have moral authority, even as he stood at the very bottom of the captain-soldier-prisoner food chain. Paul does the exact opposite of going it alone. Paul's fate could not be any more tied up in everyone else's.

With some distance, Paul's advice is utterly reasonable. In the midst of such storms, abandoning ship is a short-term solution. As soon as you have abandoned the ship, you must figure out how to deal with being tossed about without the protection of the larger vessel. So when Paul told his captors to say in the ship, to not board the life boats, he was giving them sound advice.

It is precisely Paul's constraints that give bite to his leadership. The shackles give Paul credibility in the face of difficult circumstances, and because he stands up for the right thing, even in chains, hundreds of lives are saved.

Even in shackles, Paul leads the church, and this is a good model for ministry, especially in the days of waning respect for members of the clergy and for the church in general. There was a day, I am told, in which a minister had clout simply because of his (and it was largely "his") title. There was once a day in which a minister could stand robed in a pulpit and have the congregation take seriously his thoughts about life and faith. The title had power.

The same is true for the church. There was once a time in which the church had the moral authority to speak to an issue and actually make a difference. It was the church, especially in the northern states and territories, which led the philosophical charge against slavery in the United States in the nineteenth century. The church used to have an unassailable voice on social issues, let alone the life of faith, but now there seem to be so many voices that the cacophony itself is oppressive.

As someone new to ministry, I am offered stories of the church's moral role, and yet there is little left to back up this witness. All the studies I have seen show the church shackled to its own reputation as shallow, self-absorbed, and hypocritical. A survey conducted by Scientific American magazine in 2010 asked the question, "Whom do you typically trust to provide accurate information about important issues in society?" Of all the groups listed as options, religious authorities ranked dead last.

Dead. Last.

In a world in which the church is chained to its reputation—deserved or not—surely God does not expect us to simply remain fastened to our chains: quiet, subservient, and resigned to our fate. If Paul had remained quiet, hundreds of people would have died. In spite of his chains—no, because of his chains!—Paul was able to testify to the power of God and keep hundreds of people from abandoning their only refuge from the storm.

I suppose I am allowed to make comments like, "If I did not have to deal with my chains, I could be a real leader." But I am left to wonder what real leadership I would miss out on were I to lead without chains. Paul led from within his shackles, and so it was that all were brought safely to land.

## Questions for reflection:

1. What are the constraints holding you back from living a richer life of faith? How might you serve God from where you are?

2. The words of the oppressed have power. Do you know anyone who has suffered from oppression? What word might they speak to your church?

LESSONS FOR TODAY'S DISCIPLES

# The End?
Acts 28

> *He lived there for two whole years at his own expense and welcomed all who came to him, proclaiming the kingdom of God and teaching about the Lord Jesus Christ with all boldness and without hindrance.*

This is how Luke ends his epic story of the disciples figuring out how to become the church after the Resurrection. The grand story that began with an angel of the Lord ends with, well, nothing. We are cordially invited to twist in the wind. The story just stops, like a book that has run out of pages or a recording that cuts out before the final scene. Paul welcomed others, proclaimed the word, and taught about Christ, and just as we seem to be getting to the good part, Luke just quits writing.

Now, as every freshman writing student knows, you have got to have an ending. You cannot just stop. You have to have some sort of end, some sort of resolution. Without the ending, the reader turns the page and finds, well, nothing.

After all, even life has an ending. We live for a time, and then we die, and that is the end of it. If I am to tell the story of my grandfather, his death is a necessary, if sad, part of the story. Death is not the most important part of the story, but it is part of the story. Even good stories must end.

Acts, however, does not end. At least, it does not end in a way that gives me any feeling of resolution. It just sort of keeps going, though not because we do not have any idea about what happened next.

We do, in fact, have a pretty good idea of what happened after Paul's two years of preaching. What is not said in Acts is that after he preached for another couple of years, Paul was most likely killed, beheaded as was his privilege as a Roman Citizen, though it does not seem like such a great privilege to me. Paul's death is part of his story, even if Luke does not write it down, preferring for whatever reason to leave the Book of Acts a cliffhanger forever. I do not know what Luke was thinking when he simply neglected to finish the book. Luke's other book, his Gospel, ends dramatically, with Jesus's speech to his disciples, followed by the Ascension and Luke's acknowledgement that even after Jesus was no longer physically present with them, the disciples responded with joy.

You can easily trace the narrative arc of the Gospel: Jesus is born, Jesus lives and teaches, Jesus dies, Jesus rises, disciples rejoice. That is a real story.

Acts has no such arc, and the lack of an ending may itself be the point, especially when measured next to Paul's continued work. Though he is imprisoned, and though he has lost his freedom, Paul continues to work for the sake of the Gospel. If the letters of Paul and his story in Acts are any guide, Paul is no fool. He is many things, but he is no fool. Paul knew what awaited him. Death was the only option. Not even his silver tongue could save him.

In the face of certain death, Paul just kept going, teaching and preaching and going about doing the business of the kingdom of God. It was as if Paul knew that the grand story in which he found himself was not, at the end of the day, about him at all. It was as if Paul knew that the story which began with an angel would not, in fact, end with him. Though Paul carried something very precious, though he was entrusted with carrying the mission of the church for a time, he knew that the mission would not end with him. The mission was much larger than one person. It could not be dragged to the bottom of the sea. It could not be locked up in a cramped, mildewed cell. It could not be left for dead on an island. The mission was larger.

So Luke leaves Paul preaching and teaching. No use focusing on the death, because while there is something to be said for Paul's courage, it is the continuing that matters. The ultimate business of Acts is the establishment of the Church, and while we do often speak of death in the church, we do not speak of death for death's sake. We speak of death as it relates to resurrection, as it relates to the continuing of God's Spirit in the world, as it relates to God's call to continue being about the work of the kingdom of God.

Paul was killed. Though this fact is not written into the story, you will find it in the footnotes. But Paul's death, though tragic, was not the end of the story. For the story of the church is one of resurrection, such that neither a cell nor an executioner's axe could stop the story.

After Paul, others welcomed the stranger in the name of God and in Paul's memory, teaching and proclaiming the word of God in places of which Paul had never even heard. After Paul, others came, including Luke himself, to tell the story and continue the work. Some of those who came later died because of their beliefs. Some survived the trails of faith and died after long, fruitful lives. Some continue still. The story has not yet ended.

I have heard it said that the church is always one generation away from extinction. I would simply add that I am far less concerned about the church simply ceasing to exist because of some sort of lack of interest in eternal matters than I am about the church dying because God's people decide that the story is over. The ending is not ours to write, and when we insert an ending just because it makes more sense that way, we are not doing justice to God's story, to the story that in some ways began with an angel but in other ways began much earlier and has in its inception traces of the breath of God.

It is easier to end the story, of course. It is much easier to declare that everything has been finished. It keeps us from having to take part in keeping the story alive. We say that the story is finished, that we will receive our reward, and we use whatever ending we have created to prove our points and win our arguments. It is much easier to end the story early. It keeps us from having to fully participate in it.

The Book of Acts is full of people who knew that the story was bigger than their own lives. Peter sold everything he owned to lead a group of earnest but thoroughly human disciples on an unpredictable adventure. Ananias went to look after a murderer, against his better judgment. Even certain death could not make Paul retreat within himself. There is no earthly logic that demands this sort of commitment; the law of self-preservation forbids it. And yet . . .

The story of God was bigger than this entire cast of characters. It continues to be bigger. There is no ending to this story, at least not yet, because the story is not over yet. So go ahead and add your piece to this grand story. Claim your spot. Keep writing. God is depending upon it.

## Questions for reflection:

1. How are you continuing God's story in your own life?

2. How can the church continue God's story?

# About the Author

The Rev. Dalton Troy Rushing is a provisional elder in the North Georgia Conference of the United Methodist Church, where he serves as Pastor of Serve (associate) at Johns Creek United Methodist Church. His blog, The Inside Out Life, can be found at www.daltonrushing.com. Dalton and his wife, the Rev. Stacey Rushing, serve on church staff together as a clergy couple. They live with their daughter in Duluth, Georgia.